# THINGS PEOPLE SAY
# ABOUT DETROIT
## A COLLECTION OF QUOTES AS TOLD TO

THE *Nain Rouge*

**DAVE KRIEGER**

THINGS PEOPLE SAY ABOUT DETROIT
A COLLECTION OF QUOTES AS TOLD TO THE NAIN ROUGE
www. thenainrouge.net

Text ©2017 Dave Krieger
Design ©2017 KMW studio publishing LLC

First Edition, 2018
Published and designed by KMW studio publishing, New York
www.kmwstudio.com

For information: contact@kmwstudio.com

ISBN: 978-0-9973916-6-4

Printed in Italy

# CONTENTS

# PREFACE

By John G. Rodwan, Jr.

Soon after Antoine de la Mothe Cadillac first set foot near the spot on the Detroit River where Hart Plaza was eventually constructed, he spied a red dwarf he'd been warned would cause his downfall. And that turned out to be the case, as Cadillac eventually left the city he'd founded in 1701 and died broke and humiliated back in France. Ever since, that crimson devil – the Nain Rouge – has been blamed for every setback Detroit suffered, from the fire of 1805 to the riots of 1943 to the rebellion of 1967. Some Detroiters came to believe that if they could chase the Nain Rouge out of town, as Cadillac unsuccessfully attempted to do, then living would be easy and their good fortune assured.

That's the legend, anyway, and there's even a bit of truth to it. The Nain Rouge was in Detroit at the very beginning. He did witness pivotal moments of Detroit's history. And the dude is red.

But here's the thing: far from masterminding devastation and engineering municipal demise, the Nain Rouge is the ultimate Detroit booster. Over the course of more than three centuries, he's befriended Detroiters both prominent and obscure and supported their efforts to develop the city, help it thrive, and recover from various troubles for which he's wholly blameless.

And while I'm debunking false stories, I might as well set the record straight on another matter. I've heard it suggested that the Nain Rouge is really just a mouthpiece for another fellow Detroiter, Dave Krieger. They did collaborate on another book, *Things I Do in Detroit: A Guidebook to the Coolest Places by the Nain Rouge*, for which Dave took photographs. And the two share a wicked sense of humor and an unfiltered outspokenness.

In the pages that follow, the Nain Rouge gathers things said by some of the many people he's encountered over the years. Some are lifelong Detroiters, some lived here for a time but ended up elsewhere, and some merely visited. But all had something to say about the city. Through these quotes, and memories and reflections from the Nain Rouge, a sort of oral history of the city tells a very different story than the one usually heard – story of a city characterized by tenacity, humor, industriousness, creativity, deviousness, and dedication.

Which explains why you couldn't chase the Nain Rouge out of Detroit if you tried.

*John G. Rodwan, Jr., is the author of Holidays & Other Disasters, which deliberately says nothing about the Marche du Nain Rouge, and the co-author of Detroit Is: An Essay in Photographs.*

# INTRODUCTION

*"Now, now, lay off Detroit.*
*Them people is livin' in Mad Max times."*

- Moe Szyslak, *The Simpsons*

Over the years, Detroit has been ridiculed, derided and portrayed as a bastion of crime, neglect and failure. Despite the fact Detroit has three-quarters of a million residents that live, work and play here, it is regarded as abandoned and forgotten. For those of us who call Detroit home, for those who have lived here for a time and moved elsewhere, and for those who find affinity with Detroit, here are some sentiments I have assembled throughout the year that reflect the true Detroit.

I hope this collection of quotes and reflections from Detroiters and those who have visited can offer inspiration, reflection and some comedy to you. And if it doesn't, then to hell with you, because you'll never understand the city I love and where I've lived from day one.

*Nain Rouge*

# ON DETROIT PEOPLE

*"Life without risks is not worth living."*
- Charles Lindbergh, Aviator

Detroit has raised a hell of a lot of talented people. Whether they remain or search out their dreams in other cities, one bond that never breaks is their lessons learned in Detroit. Here are some witticisms from those who called Detroit home.

**Mitch Albom (1958- ), Author and Detroit Free Press Columnist,** is an advocate for the disenfranchised in Detroit: former autoworkers, high school dropouts, and ordinary folks who have been ignored or have been left behind in this new economy.

*"Detroit is a place where we've had it pretty tough. But there is a generosity here and a well of kindness that goes deep."*

I believe Mitch is the real deal. He came to Detroit as a sportswriter, but he has embraced our town and made it his mission to improve the conditions for those less fortunate.

**Tim Allen (1953- ), Actor,** grew up in suburban Detroit, graduating from Birmingham Seaholm High School. On a dare, Allen began doing standup comedy at Mark Ridley's Comedy Castle, where he gained notoriety.

*"If you don't decide where you're going, life will decide for you."*

*"A guy knows he's in love when he loses interest in his car for a couple of days."*

*"My mom said the only reason men are alive is for lawn care and vehicle maintenance."*

Known for his television show *Home Improvement*, Allen is also the voice of Buzz Lightyear.

**Mike Binder (1958- ), Actor and Director,** grew up in Detroit and started his career as a comedian.

*"I'm not a New Yorker. I grew up in Detroit. A lot of people think it's one big city but they're completely different."*

Mike won a few awards for his work in Hollywood and directs most of the screenplays he writes.

**Grace Lee Boggs, (1915-2015), Social Activist,** was a life-long proponent of Detroit. Her commentaries on Detroit are legendary.

*"I think Detroit is already providing a model for change in the world. I think that Detroit – I mean, people come from all over the world to see what we're doing. People are looking for a new way of living."*

Grace had insight into many things but always offered a fascinating look at what was going on in our city before we could recognize it.

**William Boeing, (1881-1956), Aviation Executive,** was a native Detroiter. Boeing's father made a fortune in lumber in northern Michigan. Moving to Seattle, William, following his father's footsteps, invested in lumber in the Pacific Northwest. Fascinated with airplanes after seeing one in a 1909 air show, Boeing became a pilot.

*"Hard work can lick what appear to be insurmountable difficulties."*

Boeing decided that he could build a better airplane. In 1916, he made his first plane, the Boeing Model 1.

**George Armstrong Custer (1839-1876), Military General,** came to Detroit for the dedication of the Soldiers and Sailors Monument in 1872. His cavalry routed Jeb Stuart's at Gettysburg, leading to a Union victory. I told him that there were great opportunities out west.

*"Where did all these damn Indians come from?"*

It didn't go so well for him. Custer was routed and killed in the Battle of the Little Bighorn.

**Erin Cummings (1977- ), Actor,** came to Detroit to film the TV show *Detroit 187* in 2010.

*"I can read in any book and newspaper about the city of Detroit, but I want to hear what the people in Detroit have to say about Detroit. My best education is actually talking to people."*

Enchanted with the city, she founded "Mittens for Detroit," an initiative that distributes gloves and mittens to children in Detroit.

**Wayne Dyer, (1940-2015), Philosopher,** grew up in an orphanage on Detroit's east side. A graduate of Denby High School and Wayne State University, Dyer has authored many self-help books.

*"I grew up in the east side of Detroit, in an area where there was very little, except for a lot of scarcity, poverty and hunger. Even growing up in an orphanage, I never woke up saying, 'I'm an orphan again today, isn't this terrible? Poor me.'"*

Using his early life experiences, Dyer's message of self-actualization resonates with his audience.

**Marc Djozlija (1967- ), Chef,** has opened some of the best restaurants around town. His grandma used to tell him every day-

*"People are fucking stupid."*

I'm not sure if he feels that way but he was proud enough of her to tell me about it and I thought it funny enough to add it here.

**Michael Eric Dyson (1958- ), Professor,** graduated from Northwestern High School and has written over a dozen books on African-American history and events.

*"I was born in '58, so the riot in Detroit in 1967 was a memorable introduction to the issue of race and*

*how race made a difference in American society. And then the next year, of course, Martin Luther King Jr.'s assassination. And the Detroit Tigers winning the World Series. All of that made a huge impression on my growing mind."*

*"I have no interest in romanticizing poor black people, having been one of them myself in our beloved hometown of Detroit."*

Dyson, a brilliant academic, is currently a Professor of Sociology at Georgetown.

**Thomas A. Edison (1847-1931), Inventor,** used to ride the rails as a young boy from Port Huron to Detroit. During an experiment in the back of a train, Edison started a fire. The conductor responding to the blaze struck him in the ears and threw him and his equipment off the train. Edison, who became partially deaf, blames this for his hearing loss.

*"The greatest invention in the world is the mind of a child."*

*"Our greatest weakness lies in giving up. The most certain way to succeed is always to try just one more time."*

*"I have not failed. I've just found 10,000 ways that won't work."*

*"The trouble with most people is that they quit before they start."*

*"Genius is one percent inspiration and ninety-nine percent perspiration."*

*"There is no substitute for hard work."*

Edison was a prolific inventor, holding more than 1,000 patents, many related to sound, because of his hearing loss. A young Henry Ford met Edison as an employee and they began a lifelong friendship.

**Keith Ellison (1963- ), Congressman, MN,** graduated from University of Detroit Jesuit High School in 1981. Ellison converted to Islam while attending Wayne State University.

*"My mom, Clida, taught my four brothers and me about her father's work to organize black voters in rural Louisiana in the 1950s. We carried her dad's legacy of activism with us. The Civil Rights Movement was present in the daily life of my family in Detroit in the 1970s."*

Ellison is the first Muslim ever elected to Congress, representing Minnesota's 5th District. He was sworn in on a Qur'an once owned by Thomas Jefferson.

**Jeffrey Eugenides (1960- ), Author,** went to University Liggett School in Grosse Pointe. Jeffrey has said he has a "perverse love" for Detroit.

*"I think the suicides in my last book came from the idea of growing up in Detroit. If you grow up in a city like that you feel everything is perishing, evanescent and going away very quickly."*

*"I think most of the major elements of American history are exemplified in Detroit, from the triumph of the automobile and the assembly line to the blight of racism, not to mention the music, Motown, the MC5, house, techno."*

Jeffrey points to his experiences growing up in Detroit as greatly influencing his writing.

**Tom Hayden (1939-2016), Political Activist,** was born in Detroit and graduated from Royal Oak Dondero High School. While attending the University of Michigan, Tom started the activist group Students for a Democratic Society, writing their manifesto, the "Port Huron Statement."

*"I was raised in an Irish-American home in Detroit where assimilation was the uppermost priority. The price of assimilation and respectability was amnesia… My parents knew nothing of this past, or nothing worth passing on."*

Hayden was one of the "Chicago Eight" protesters arrested at the 1968 Democratic Convention. He later served in the California Assembly.

**Edward Herrmann (1943-2014), Actor,** grew up in Grosse Pointe and was a noted character actor.

*"Growing up as a kid in Detroit, way back, there was a movie station that would show old kinescope reproductions of old movies, and I remember seeing Bela Lugosi for the first time and being duly frightened out of my mind."*

*"You ingest the automobile in the very air of Detroit, or at least you did in the 1940s and 1950s."*

Detroit's automotive heritage led to Edward's

enthusiasm for collecting classic cars. He was a regular master of ceremonies for the annual Pebble Beach Concours d'Elegance, and restored a few classics himself.

**Emily Gail, (1946- ) Detroit Advocate,** had a store downtown that was an eclectic mix of everything fun: video games, tchotkes and trinkets of all sorts, many with a Detroit origin. It was a true reflection of her passion for Detroit. Her slogan became ubiquitous:

*"Say nice things about Detroit."*

Emily was a fixture in the 1970s; she single-handedly promoted Detroit and inspired us to embrace our city when it seemed everyone was fleeing to the suburbs.

**Jerry Herron, (1949- ) Author and Wayne State University Professor,** is from Texas and such men don't sugarcoat things.

*"Detroit is just like everywhere else, only more so – a lot more so."*

His book *After Culture: Detroit and the Humiliation of History* is a great dive into the soul of Detroit.

**Keegan-Michael Key (1971- ), Actor,** was raised in Detroit and went to Royal Oak Shrine High School and the University of Detroit Mercy. A founder of Planet Ant Theatre in Hamtramck, he was a member of Detroit's Second City cast and co-founded the Detroit Creativity Project, which teaches Detroit students improvisation in order to improve their communication skills.

*"Some of the friendliest, friendliest people you're going to meet are going to be in Detroit."*

*"And people don't understand when they come to Detroit, it's not that we were a music town. We are a music town. We are an art town. We boast one of the greatest art institutes on planet Earth."*

*"Everybody used to have the T-shirts that used to say, "Detroit: Where the weak are killed and eaten." It's so funny because we're one of the first places in the United States of America that experienced branding. It wasn't good branding, but it was branding. I think in the last 30 years, we've turned it around, so the branding is positive."*

Key also performs with the 313, an improv group of former residents of Detroit's 313 area code.

**Sebastian Spering Kresge (1867-1966), Executive,** began his Kresge 5 and 10 cent store in 1897, selling cheap wares on Woodward. By 1924, he was worth $6 billion in today's dollars.

*"Money alone cannot build character or transform evil into good. It cries for full partnership with leaders of character and good will who value good tools in the creation and enlargement of life for Man."*

In 1962, Kresge opened the first K Mart store becoming the second largest retailer in the country through the 1980s.

**Charlie LeDuff  (1966- ), Author,** is a Pulitzer Prize winner who has exposed the corruption, incompetence and failures of our city's leaders through his investigative journalism.

*"Go ahead and laugh at Detroit. Because you are laughing at yourself."*

Charlie writes with a focused humor. His compassion for the everyman, just trying to get along, and his intolerance for corruption in the political class drives his work.

**Elmore "Dutch" Leonard (1925-2013), Author,** a graduate of the University of Detroit, is considered the "Dickens of Detroit" for his honest portrayals of his hometown.

*"There are cities that get by on their good looks, or their climate and scenery, views of mountains or oceans, rockbound or with palm trees. And there are cities like Detroit that have to work for a living."*

I knew "Dutch" when he was a copywriter for Campbell Ewald, a famed Detroit ad agency where he honed his narrative skills.

**Charles Lindbergh (1902-1874), Aviator,** was born in Detroit and early on was fascinated with flight. Nicknamed "Lucky Lindy," Charles flew out of obscurity by piloting the *Spirit of St. Louis* across the Atlantic solo, becoming the first pilot to do so.

*"I never had a dull moment at Detroit."*

*"Success is not measured by what a man accomplishes, but by the opposition he has encountered and the courage with which he has maintained the struggle against overwhelming odds."*

*"Isn't it strange that we talk least about the things we think about most?"*

*"Whatever a man imagines, he can achieve."*

His mother, Evangeline Lindbergh, was a chemistry teacher at Cass Technical High School.

**The Lone Ranger (1933-  ),** was a fictional character who became a national hero in the early days of radio. Started in Detroit at WXYZ, The Lone Ranger was known for its music from the "William Tell Overture" and the introduction- "With his faithful Indian companion, Tonto, the daring and resourceful masked rider of the plains led the fight for law and order in the early West. Return with us now to those thrilling days of yesteryear. The Lone Ranger rides again!"

*"Come on, Silver! Let's go, big fellow! Hi-yo, Silver! Away!"*

*"Don't worry about this mask, it's on the side of the law."*

*"I don't shoot to kill. I want a silver bullet to be a symbol of justice."*

The Lone Ranger was conceived by George Trendle, the station owner, and Fran Striker, the writer, as a children's show but more than half the audience who tuned in were adults. Another one of their hit shows, *The Green Hornet*, was introduced around the same time.

**Joyce Carol Oates (1938- ), Novelist,** began her career teaching at the University of Detroit Mercy while living in a Palmer Park apartment. For the next twenty years, living around the Detroit area, she became a prolific writer, earning many awards.

*"Detroit, my 'great' subject, made me the person I am, consequently the writer I am – for better or worse."*

Using Detroit as her muse, Oates credits her time spent in Detroit during the tumultuous 1960s as inspiration for her work. I think *Them* is one of her best novels.

**Jeanette Pierce (1981- ), Advocate,** through her efforts at the Detroit Experience Factory, is changing minds and challenging the false narrative of Detroit, created over decades by the national media and politicians who have disparaged us.

*"Detroit is big enough to matter in the world and small enough for you to matter in it."*

Jeanette has been a friend and advocate ever since she came to Detroit. I love her passion and intuition about what Detroit is and could become.

**Gilda Radner (1946-1989), Actor,** attended University Liggett School and University of Michigan, dropping out her senior year. Gilda spent her youth at her father's hotel where she met many nightclub performers who were performing in town.

*"I'd much rather be a woman than a man. Women can cry, they can wear cute clothes, and they're the first to be rescued off sinking ships."*

*"I can always be distracted by love, but eventually I get horny for my creativity."*

*"Life is about not knowing, having to change, taking the moment and making the best of it, without knowing what's going to happen next."*

*"Dreams are like paper, they tear so easily."*

Gilda went on to become a member of Second City in Toronto then on to *Saturday Night Live*.

**Mitt Romney (1947- ), Executive,** grew up in Palmer Woods and went on to study at Cranbrook. His father became governor of Michigan, and following Dad's lead, Mitt became Governor of Massachusetts.

*"I'm a son of Detroit. I was born in Detroit."*

I've never really heard Mitt say anything about Detroit until he started running for president and spoke about how lovely the trees were here.

**Soupy Sales (1926-2009), Comic and TV Personality,** was born Milton Supman in North Carolina and came to Detroit in 1953 working for WXYZ-TV, beginning his famous children's show *Lunch with Soupy Sales*.

*"What starts with 'F' and ends with 'UCK'? A firetruck!"*

*"I climbed up a tree and kissed my girl between the limbs."*

*"I took my wife to a baseball game - I kissed her on the strikes, and she kissed me on the balls."*

Known for his off-color wit and comedy, Sales developed his style while in Detroit. His famous cream pie routine began when I hit him in the face with a pie after he made a joke about my appearance. We laughed our asses off.

**George C. Scott (1927-1999), Actor,** graduated from Redford High School and went on to become one of America's great actors. His portrayal of Patton won him an Oscar in 1970.

*"There is no question you get pumped up by the recognition. Then a self-loathing sets in when you realize you're enjoying it."*

*"Truth is not always a pleasant thing."*

*"I think you have to be schizoid three different ways to be an actor ... You have to be a human being. Then you have to be the character you're playing. And on top of that you've got to be the guy sitting out there in Row 10, watching yourself and judging yourself. That's why most of us are crazy to start with, or go nuts once we get into it."*

Rejecting his Oscar, George felt that you couldn't compare roles as every performance is unique.

**Tom Selleck (1946-   ), Actor,** was born in Detroit and spent his early childhood here before moving to southern California.

*"I had a strong, really good upbringing, not puritanical."*

*"Hopefully you marry someone who you not only love, but who you like as well."*

A lifelong Detroit Tigers fan, Selleck was noted for always wearing a Tigers cap on the television show *Magnum PI*.

**J.K. Simons (1946- ), Actor,** grew up in Grosse Pointe, son of a family of teachers. He has become a noted character actor and won an Oscar for his role in *Whiplash*.

*"Things heal. Bad stuff happens, but you go on. Life takes care of it."*

*"People evolve and it's important to not stop evolving just because you've reached 'adulthood.'"*

*"If you are lucky enough to have a parent or two alive on this planet, call them. Don't text; don't e-mail. Call them on the phone."*

An avid Tigers fan, J.K. played the Detroit Tigers manager in the movie *For Love of the Game*.

**Lily Tomlin (1939- ), Actor,** graduated from Cass Tech High School and attended Wayne State University. Starting her career as a comedian, Tomlin won a Grammy for her first comedy album *This Is a Recording*, in 1972.

*"The trouble with the rat race is that even if you win, you're still a rat."*

*"I always wondered why somebody doesn't do something about that. Then I realized I was somebody."*

*"Wouldn't it be great if we all grew up to be what we wanted to be? The world would be full of nurses, firemen, and ballerinas."*

*"I like a teacher who gives you something to take home to think about besides homework."*

*"The start to a better world is the belief that it is possible."*

Lily's thoughts on life are as funny as the characters she plays.

**Robin Williams (1951-2014), Actor,** moved to Bloomfield Hills at the age of 12. He attended Detroit Country Day School, becoming class president.

*"I used to think that the worst thing in life was to end up alone. It's not. The worst thing in life is to end up with people who make you feel alone."*

*"No matter what people tell you, words and ideas can change the world."*

*"Comedy can be a cathartic way to deal with personal trauma."*

Robin went on to become one of the greatest comics of his generation.

**Darren Walker (1960- ), Director, Ford Foundation,** led the Ford Foundation's efforts during Detroit's bankruptcy, negotiating "The Grand Bargain," raising funds to save the DIA and city employee pensions.

*"Detroit is a metaphor for America, for America's challenges and America's opportunities. It is a hothouse for new innovation, for ingenuity and risk taking. That doesn't happen in a lot of American cities. We need to be in Detroit because of that."*

For years the Ford Foundation, which was head-quartered in Detroit, and funded with the hard work of Detroiters, neglected the city. Walker has resolved to make the Ford Foundation more active in contributing to Detroit's needs.

**Steven Yeun (1983- ), Actor,** was raised in suburban Detroit and found fame as Glenn Rhee on *The Walking Dead*.

*"People think that Detroit is this barren wasteland. While there are parts that are not as nice as others, the misconception is not true. It is definitely not a thriving community in Detroit, but it is getting there. There is a lot of heart and love in this city."*

Born Jeun Yeun in South Korea, Yeun's parents changed his name to Steven, after meeting a local doctor of the same name.

# ON THE AUTO INDUSTRY

*"History is more or less bunk."*
- Henry Ford, Industrialist

Detroit was a leader in many industries before and after the invention of the automobile, but the auto industry has come to represent Detroit, and Detroit has become synonymous with the automobile. Many of these quotes are from friends. I hung out with most of the early industry leaders and I handpicked some of their best.

**Grace Lee Boggs (1915-2015), Social Activist,** advocated for union representation in the auto companies. Her writings about capitalism and workers' rights were instrumental in the union movement.

*"The standardization and specialization of industrialization was being undermined by globalization. When people in Bangladesh could produce things much more cheaply than anybody could produce them in Detroit, we no longer were the world capital of industrialization."*

*"I think Detroit shows that we've come to the end of the industrial epoch and have to find a new mode of production."*

Grace dedicated her life towards enriching Detroit and its citizens.

**Louis-Joseph "Louie" Chevrolet (1878-1941), Race Car Driver and Co-founder of Chevrolet,** emigrated from Switzerland becoming a race car driver for Fiat. Louis went on to race for Buick in his early years, befriending Billy Durant, founder of General Motors. Together, they formed the Chevrolet Motor Company in 1911.

*"Movement is the universal language of personal freedom."*

Louis raced in the Indy 500 four times with cars he designed. Louis was a fascinating personality; he loved fast cars and his aggressive innovations were motivated by speed.

**Walter Chrysler (1875-1940), Executive,** began his career at Buick. Chrysler acquired the Maxwell Motor Company in 1921, changing the name to the Chrysler Corporation, and added Plymouth and DeSoto to his list of brands. In 1928, he purchased the Dodge name.

*"I feel sorry for the person who can't get genuinely excited about his work. Not only will he never be satisfied, but he will never achieve anything worthwhile."*

*"The reason so many people never get anywhere in life is because when opportunity knocks, they are out in the backyard looking for four-leaf clovers."*

*"To me every hour of the day and night is an unspeakably perfect miracle."*

*"The real secret of success is enthusiasm."*

More a banker then a visionary, Chrysler had the management skills many of the early automakers lacked.

**John DeLorean, (1925-2005), Designer and Executive,** went to Cass Tech and graduated from Lawrence Tech University. Beginning his engineering career at Packard, he was a bright star in a failing company. Joining Pontiac, DeLorean rose to become the youngest division head in GM history. While at Pontiac, he transformed a bland division into GM's performance division, introducing the GTO and Firebird.

*"We seem to forget that a cloistered executive, whose only social contacts are with similar executives who make $500,000 a year, and who has not really bought a car the way a customer has in years, has no basis to judge public taste."*

*"There were and are men in positions of power at GM who do not know the business they are running. Many were not good businessmen in the areas with which they are familiar."*

*"A car should make people's eyes light up when they step into the showroom."*

DeLorean was an eccentric for Detroit at the time. His bravado was unaccepted by the corporate chiefs. John left GM and started his own company, the DeLorean Motor Company. Unfortunately, his dream died when he tried to save the company with a cocaine deal. His car lives on in the *Back to the Future* movies.

**John Francis Dodge (1864-1920), Machinist,** and his brother, Horace, were inseparable. Setting up a machine shop in 1902, they began making parts for the Olds Motor Company, moving to Ford in 1907 to build engines. After ten years, the brothers left Ford and started the Dodge Brothers Company in Hamtramck.

*"If you think you can do a thing or think you can't do a thing, you're right."*

*"We're brothers and we always work together…"*

The brothers were always seen as outcasts from Detroit's moneyed class. When John contracted influenza in New York City, in 1918, and died a year later, his untimely death hit Horace hard. Horace passed away less than a year later.

**Harley Earl (1894-1969), Designer,** founded the Earl Automotive Works in Hollywood, in 1908, making car bodies for movie stars. Lawrence Fisher of Cadillac, commissioned Earl to design the 1927 LaSalle. Earl became the first director of the Art and Color Section, designing bodies for all GM autos. Prior to this, most manufacturers shipped chassis to a coach builder of the buyer's choice.

*"The art of automobile design has progressed, until today it is regarded as one of the most important factors in the marketing of the automobile."*

Earl left a huge legacy at GM as the originator of clay modeling, the wraparound windshield, the hardtop sedan, two-tone paint and tailfins. His design influence led GM to become the largest corporation in the world when he retired.

**Harvey Firestone (1868-1938), Manufacturer,** was a close friend of Henry Ford and founder of the Firestone Tire and Rubber Company, one of the first global tire makers.

*"Success is the sum of details."*

Along with Ford and Thomas Edison, Firestone was a member of the "Millionaires' Club," an exclusive group of industrial leaders that would vacation together.

**Henry Ford (1863-1947), Industrialist,** began working in 1891 at the Edison Illuminating Company, beginning a lifelong friendship with his mentor, Thomas Edison. His Model T revolutionized America, marketing a low-cost automobile to the masses for the first time. His "$5 a day" offer to employees reduced the turnover rate, allowing for better, trained workers. Ford also introduced the "40-hour work week" believing that a well-rested workforce performed better, also conceding that well-paid workers would consume more goods on their off days.

*"Any customer can have a car painted any color that he wants so long as it is black."*

*"Quality means doing it right when no one is looking."*

*"You can't build a reputation on what you are going to do."*

*"It is not the employer who pays the wages. Employers only handle the money. It is the customer who pays wages."*

*"Thinking is the hardest work there is, which is probably the reason why so few engage in it."*

*"I am looking for a lot of men who have an infinite capacity to not know what can't be done."*

*"What's right about America is that although we have a mess of problems, we have great capacity – intellect and resources – to do something about them."*

*"Most people spend more time and energy going around problems than in trying to solve them."*

Ford believed in global expansion and that international trade and cooperation led to international peace. The Rouge Complex, begun in 1917, the world's largest manufacturing complex, fulfilled Ford's goal to produce a vehicle from scratch in a single factory.

**Edsel Ford (1893-1943), Designer and Executive,** as a boy used to work with his father in an attic above their garage, learning to master the skills of building by hand. Groomed to take over the business, Edsel desired to develop more stylish cars than the Model T. He purchased Lincoln Motors in 1922 and founded the Mercury division of Ford in 1938. Credited with the design of the 1939 Lincoln Continental, one of the most inspiring cars ever, he originally intended it as his personal car. For a while, I had one myself.

*"Father made the most popular cars in the world; I want to make the best."*

*"There are no crown princes at Ford."*

The most graceful and gracious of the auto barons, Edsel loved art and design and was a major benefactor for the arts in Detroit. His famous commission, "Detroit Industry" by Diego Rivera, in the Detroit Institute of Arts, is a masterpiece – a monumental set of murals depicting the assembly line.

**Henry Ford II (1917-1987), Executive,** was the third generation of Fords to lead the company. Taking over in 1945, "Hank the Deuce" brought with him the "Whiz Kids," young executives intent on turning around the company.

*"The first qualification for success in my view is a strong work ethic."*

*"We can't take a slipshod and easygoing attitude toward education in this country. And by 'we' I don't mean 'somebody else,' but I mean me and I mean you. It is the future of our country – yours and mine – which is at stake."*

Speaking about his public dispute with Ford President Lee Iacocca, whom he fired in 1978, Henry said:

*"Sometimes you just don't like somebody."*

Gifted with the determination of the elder Henry, Hank led Ford to success in the post-war era. Despite his leadership similarities with his grandfather, Hank hated the way Henry treated Edsel, who was a loving father, kind and soft spoken.

**Bill Ford (1957- ), Executive,** is the great-grandson of Henry Ford and Harvey Firestone. Beginning at Ford in 1979, Ford became Chairman of the Board in 1998, continuing the family governance legacy.

*"As long as gas is cheaper than bottled water, we can't be in a position of dictating to the consumer what to buy."*

After the 1999 Rouge Powerhouse explosion that killed six workers and injured dozens, a staffer remarked to Bill, "Generals don't go out to the front lines." He responded:

*"Then bust me down to private."*

Despite his family's storied place in Detroit history, Bill is much more casual and relaxed. His pro-environment beliefs are reflected in the new technology at the Rouge Complex.

**James "Jimmy" Hoffa (1930-1975?), Union Activist,** became active in the labor movement in his teenage years while working at a grocery store. He defiantly led the workers to organize and was fired by the chain, leading to his role with the Teamsters. Led by Hoffa and other leaders, the union saw membership rise from 75,000 in 1933 to more than a million in 1951.

*"I do to others what they do to me, only worse."*

*"I may have my faults, but being wrong ain't one of them."*

*"I've said consistently that no employer ever really accepts a union. They tolerate the unions. The very minute they can get a pool of unemployment they'll challenge the unions and try to get back what they call managements prerogatives, meaning hire, fire, pay what you want."*

Jimmy became Teamster President in 1958, leading the union for the next decade. Convicted of bribery and fraud, Hoffa was sent to prison in 1967. After his release in 1971, Hoffa tried to regain control over the union. For decades, Hoffa and the Teamsters were accused of alleged organized crime ties. On July 30, 1975, after arriving for a reputed meeting with noted Mafia figures, Anthony Giacalone and Anthony Provenzano, Jimmy disappeared.

**Lee Iacocca (1924- ), Executive,** joined Ford in 1946, becoming President in 1970. Iacocca became CEO of Chrysler in 1978, leading the company out of a potential bankruptcy by receiving a loan guarantee from the U.S. government, thereby saving the company.

*"You can have brilliant ideas, but if you can't get them across, your ideas won't get you anywhere."*

*"Over the years, many executives have said to me with pride: 'Boy, I worked so hard last year that I didn't take any vacation.' I always feel like responding, 'You dummy. You mean to tell me you can take responsibility for an eighty-million-dollar project and you can't plan two weeks out of the year to have some fun?'"*

*"Listening can make the difference between a mediocre organization and a great one."*

*"The right decision is the wrong decision if it's made too late."*

*"If you can find a better car buy it."*

After introducing America to the minivan, Lee became the face for Chrysler.

**John F. Kennedy (1917-1963), President, (1961-1963),** was a strong advocate for union workers. Under his administration, his fiscal policies brought 5.5% GDP growth, and kept inflation at 1%.

*"Collective bargaining has always been the bedrock of the American labor movement. I hope that you will continue to anchor your movement to this foundation. Free collective bargaining is good for the entire Nation. In my view, it is the only alternative to State regulation of wages and prices – a path which leads far down the grim road of totalitarianism. Those who would destroy or further limit the rights of organized labor – those who would cripple collective bargaining or prevent organization of the unorganized – do a disservice to the cause of democracy."*

The promise of a progressive leader for the United States was cut short but his legacy remains as a strong leader for the working and middle classes.

**Charles Kettering (1876-1958), Engineer,** holds more than 186 patents and was founder of Delco which, in 1912, developed the self-starter for autos, rendering the hand crank obsolete. Kettering was head of research at GM from 1920 to 1947.

*"99 percent of success is built on failure."*

*"I am not interested in the past. I am interested in the future, for that is where I expect to spend the rest of my life."*

*"If you're doing something the same way you have been doing it for ten years, the chances are you are doing it wrong."*

Described as one of the Gods of the automotive field, Kettering excelled at inventing new products to make cars safer and more comfortable.

**Bob Lutz (1932- ), Executive,** worked at all three of Detroit's auto companies at one time or another, rising to Vice-Chairman of Product Development at GM.

*"Being able to 'think out of the box' presupposes you were able to think in it."*

*"Design can be both a manifestation of a company's design ethic and an outward communication of a company's design ethic and drive for excellence."*

An expert in understanding the customer's desire, he is considered a "car guy," one who loves the experience of driving a well-made car.

**Ransom E. Olds (1864-1950), Industrialist,** is said to have built his first car in 1894. Founding the Olds Motor Vehicle Company in 1897, Ransom built and sold electric, steam-powered and gasoline-powered cars – the only one to produce all three modes. The true creator of the modern assembly line, he built the first mass-produced car, the Oldsmobile Curved Dash, in 1901. To showcase his car at the New York Auto Show, he wanted to make a sale splash. When one dealer offered to purchase 500, Olds responded:

*"I would like to see you make this order for a thousand cars. Then the public would drop its jaw and take notice."*

Sealing the deal, he achieved a public-relations hit, driving sales. Removed from his own company in 1904, Ransom formed REO Motor Car Company in Lansing.

**Walter Reuther (1907-1970), Union Activist,** was a union organizer and founder of the United Auto Workers (UAW) in 1935. A prominent leader of the progressive left, Reuther was always a proponent of workers' rights.

*"If you're not big enough to lose, you're not big enough to win."*

*"In the old days, all you needed was a handshake. Nowadays you need forty lawyers."*

*"There's a direct relationship between the ballot box and the bread box, and what the union fights for and wins at the bargaining table can be taken away in the legislative halls."*

*"Labor is not fighting for a larger slice of the national pie – labor is fighting for a larger pie."*

Walter was a dominant influence in politics in his heyday. Barry Goldwater once said that he was a more "dangerous menace than the Sputnik or anything Soviet Russia might do to America," which could be taken as a compliment, in my opinion.

**Carrol Shelby (1923-2012), Race Car Driver and Designer,** began his career racing cars. In 1959, he opened a high-performance driving school and began rebuilding mass-market autos for high-performance racing. In 1964, Lee Iacocca asked Shelby to make a sports car out of the Ford Mustang. He responded:

*"Lee, you can't make a race horse out of a mule. I don't want to do it."*

But he did. Following his success with the Mustang, Shelby helped design performance cars with all of the Big Three automakers.

**Alfred Sloan (1875-1966), Executive,** became president of General Motors in 1932 and Chairman in 1937, retiring in 1954. Establishing annual styling changes, Sloan created the idea of planned obsolescence. He transformed GM's brands, creating a price hierarchy so each division wouldn't compete for the same buyers.

*"A car for every purse and purpose."*

*"The business of business is business."*

*"It is astonishing what you can do when you have a lot of energy, ambition and plenty of ignorance."*

Sloan made GM into a leader in the industry, and the largest corporation in the world for the next seventy years.

**Roger Smith (1925-2007), Executive,** oversaw the decline of GM as its chairman from 1981 to 1990. Spending billions by diversifying, reorganizing, and modernizing, Smith continued to lose market share to competitors and never addressed the bloated corporate structure that stifled innovation.

*"Anything that you do to increase job security automatically does work for you. It makes your employees a closer part of the unit."*

Widely criticized for his leadership, Roger was ridiculed in Michael Moore's *Roger and Me*, a film about the closing of auto factories and lost jobs in Flint, Michigan, GM's original hometown.

# ON ARTS & EDUCATION

*"Failure is a bruise, not a tattoo."*
- John Sinclair, Poet

Detroit has always been an exciting home to the visual arts. It has been said that whatever happens in America, Detroit experiences it first. Detroit is an inspiration and offers independence for artists to develop their own voices. Faculty and students from the College for Creative Studies (CCS), the Cranbrook Academy of Art and other schools – as well as countless self-taught artists – have been creating provocative and innovative art and design for many, many years. Our vital art scene is one of the multitude of reasons I've made Detroit my home for more than three centuries.

**Mary Chase Perry Stratton (1867-1961), Ceramic Artist,** co-founded the Pewabic Pottery studio with Horace James Caulkin in 1903. She was introduced to art in her early teens through art classes at the original Detroit Museum of Art. She established the ceramics department at the University of Michigan and taught at Wayne State University (WSU).

*"We do not need to exploit special feats of execution nor technical specialties, in order 'to show off.' That was the manner of the yesterdays, when to do one's 'best work' meant the most elaborate treatment possible, introducing every known trick of the art on the same piece of ware. Now we know that one's 'best work' is often – rather always – his most simple yet appropriate conception, relying on the thought back of it, instead of the fanciful execution of a momentary fancy."*

At Pewabic, Mary developed iridescent glazes, which became a signature for the studio. It has been said her recipes and techniques died with her, though they just might be among the papers I've accumulated over the years.

**Albert Kahn (1869-1942), Architect,** is considered the architect of modern industry and the "architect of Detroit", forming Albert Kahn and Associates in 1895. Kahn developed the "Kahn System" or "Kahn Bar," improving the use of reinforced concrete, reducing interior supports and increasing fire suppression, which he introduced in 1903 at the Packard plant. Kahn went on to design most of Detroit's manufacturing facilities, culminating with Ford's Rouge

Plant, which employed more than 120,000 workers when it opened.

*"When I began, the real architects would design only museums, cathedrals, capitols, monuments. The office boy was considered good enough to do factory buildings. I'm still that office boy designing factories. I have no dignity to be impaired."*

As Detroit grew from a small town into the fourth-largest city in the United States, Kahn also designed some of the most iconic and beautiful buildings in Detroit, including the Fisher Building, Cadillac Place, which I still think of as the GM Building, the Detroit Athletic Club and the Detroit Free Press building.

**Wilhelm Valentiner (1880-1958), Detroit Institute of Arts Director,** became the first director of the DIA in 1924. As a result of his leadership, acquisitions, and guidance, the DIA became one of the greatest art collections in the country. Wilhelm was an avid collector of German Expressionism as the Nazis systematically destroyed the art and reputations of these artists.

*"That Detroit ultimately concentrated on automobiles could be traced to one genius, Henry Ford... But*

*that the necessary human energy for this development ment existed in Detroit could be proven through its early history... To defeat the conditions imposed by earth and sky at Detroit required intensive labor by energetic men who were not tempted by pleasure and play."*

His introduction of Edsel Ford to Diego Rivera culminated in what I consider to be the greatest artwork in Detroit.

**Diego Rivera (1886-1957), Artist,** created the masterwork of Detroit art. "Detroit Industry" depicts the Ford Motor Company Rouge factory, the greatest manufacturing facility in the world at the time. His 27 panels reveal all the elements of auto assembly and include representations of the four races and the importance of technology in manufacturing.

*"As I rode back to Detroit, a vision of Henry Ford's industrial empire kept passing before my eyes. In my ears, I heard the wonderful symphony which came from his factories where metals were shaped into tools for men's service. It was a new music, waiting for the composer with genius enough to give it communicable form."*

*"I thought of the millions of different men by whose combined labor and thought automobiles were produced, from the miners who dug the iron ore out of the earth to the railroad men and teamsters who brought the finished machines to the consumer, so that man, space, and time might be conquered, and ever-expanding victories be won against death."*

Diego's Marxist beliefs were intertwined in some aspects of the murals, which created a public outcry. Although Diego was an active socialist, he loved the admiration and adoration of Detroit's elite. The majesty of these murals resonates through today and evokes the power of labor in creating the auto industry. I can't count the hours I've spent in Rivera Court contemplating Diego's masterpiece.

**Frida Kahlo (1907-1954), Artist,** came to Detroit with her husband, Diego Rivera in 1932. An avid leftist, she felt disdain for many of the benefactors Diego worked with. Suffering a miscarriage while in Detroit, her strikingly raw and emotional work reflected the many personal events in her life.

*"The industrial part of Detroit is really the most interesting side, otherwise it's like the rest of the United States, ugly and stupid."*

*"Although I am very interested in all the industrial and mechanical development of the United States... I have seen thousands of people in the most terrible misery without anything to eat and with no place to sleep, that is what has most impressed me here, it is terrifying to see the rich having parties, day and night while thousands and thousands of people are dying of hunger."*

Despite the traumas she endured while in Detroit, her art work exploded with new energy as she experimented with new techniques and developed a more independent narrative style. I consider Frida's talents equal to Diego's, but completely different; she used her personal life as an expression of her pain, while Diego sought to illustrate his opinions through the masses' struggles.

**Pablo Davis (1916-2013), Artist,** moved from Philadelphia to Detroit after seeing an ad in a newspaper about the Diego Rivera mural. Arriving in Detroit by train, he found no one who could tell him where the museum was. When he finally found it, the guards would not let him in. As he sat on the steps in despair, a woman came out and said to him:

*"You look like you just lost your best friend."*

It was Frida Kahlo. Befriending the couple, Pablo lived and worked for Diego while he completed the mural. Later, Pablo fought in the Spanish Civil War, becoming friends with Pablo Picasso, who influenced much of his work.

**Eliel Saarinen (1873-1950), Architect,** moved from Finland to the United States in 1923 and in 1925 became the lead designer of the Cranbrook Art Academy, which had been founded by George Booth of the *Detroit News*. Under Eliel's direction, Cranbrook became an international leader for modern arts and architecture studies.

*"Art was born as a desire, not as a demand."*

*"Always design a thing by considering it in its next larger context – a chair in a room, a room in a house, a house in an environment, an environment in a city plan."*

Eliel became a leader of the International Style during the mid 20th century. His contributions establishing Cranbrook as an important design school have persisted for decades.

**Eero Saarinen (1910-1961), Architect,** grew up on the campus of the Cranbrook Academy of Art, where his father was dean and taught classes. After touring Europe and Africa, Eero joined his father's design studio in the 1930s. His first major work was the General Motors Design Center, in collaboration with his father.

*"The purpose of architecture is to shelter and enhance man's life on earth and to fulfill his belief in the nobility of his existence."*

*"Function influences but does not dictate form."*

Eero's most famous projects, the TWA terminal at New York's JFK Airport and the St. Louis Arch in Missouri, have remained some of the most influential works of the 20th century.

**Ludwig Mies van der Rohe (1886-1969), Architect,** was known for his modern approach to architecture and served as the last director of the Bauhaus, a German art school, famous for introducing modernism.

*"Less is more."*

*"Architecture begins when you place two bricks carefully together."*

Mies created the famous Lafayette Park modernist neighborhood on Detroit's near eastside – one of the nation's first urban renewal projects.

**Carl Milles (1875-1955), Sculptor,** arrived from Sweden to the Cranbrook Academy in 1931. Working alongside the Saarinens and Albert Kahn, Milles created many works on the Cranbrook campus and was recognized internationally.

*"Nothing is ugly except stupidity."*

Although his work offended some Americans' sensibilities, but not mine, Carl did create some famous works, including the "Wedding of the Waters," in St. Louis, and "The Hand of God," outside the Murphy Hall of Justice in Detroit.

**Charles (1907-1978) and Ray Eames (1912-1988), Designers,** are noted for their decades-long collaboration as furniture designers and filmmakers. Together they created one of the most influential design studios of the 20th century. At the behest of Eliel Saarinen, Charles came to Cranbrook in 1938 as the head of the Industrial Design department. Ray began studying design in 1940 at Cranbrook, collaborating with Harry Bertoia and Eero Saarinen.

*"The details are not the details. They make the design."*

*"Who ever said that pleasure wasn't functional?"*

*"To whom does design address itself: to the greatest number, to the specialist of an enlightened matter, to a privileged social class? Design addresses itself to the need."*

*"What works good is better than what looks good, because what works good lasts."*

Influenced by Eliel Saarinen's International Style of design, the Eames left Cranbrook in 1941, becoming famous for their molded plywood furniture designs.

**Florence Knoll (1917- ), Designer,** was born in Saginaw and studied at Cranbrook under Saarinen from 1934 to 1935. In 1946, she married Hans Knoll, and together they joined architecture with furniture design, becoming leaders in 20th century design.

*"I am not a decorator. The only place I decorate is my own house."*

Florence was influential in changing the design of the modern office, preferring open floor plans and uncluttered spaces.

**Harry Bertoia (1915-1978), Sculptor,** went to Cass Tech, CCS, and, in 1937 attended Cranbrook, where he met Walter Gropius, Florence Knoll, and the Eames. He taught jewelry design and metal work at Cranbrook.

*"The urge for good design is the same as the urge to go on living."*

In the mid-fifties, Harry devoted himself solely to creating sound sculptures. Producing more than 50 commissions, Bertoia also made a series of recordings of music created with his sculptures, all titled, "Sonambient."

**Marshall Fredericks (1908-1998), Sculptor,** joined the staff at the Cranbrook Academy of Art in 1932. In 1936, he was awarded his first commission for the Barbour Memorial Fountain on Belle Isle, the first of many local works. Recognized internationally, Fredericks is best known for his work in the Detroit area.

*"I tried to express the spirit of man through the deity and the family. Gradually, people began calling it 'Spirit of Detroit.'"*

*"I want more than anything in the world to do sculpture which will have real meaning for other people, many people, and might in some way encourage, inspire, or give them happiness."*

His most popular sculpture, "The Spirit of Detroit," was created for the City County Building in 1958. Believing it was his civic responsibility, Marshall donated the piece to the city for free. It has since become the iconic representation of Detroit, and one of my favorite pieces of public art.

**Keith Haring (1958-1990), Artist,** credits Walt Disney, Looney Tunes, and Dr. Seuss as his major influences. Using his art for social commentary, Haring became one of the most influential artists of the 1980s. In 1987, Keith was Artist in Residence at Cranbrook.

*"The public needs art – and it is the responsibility of a 'self-proclaimed artist' to realize that the public needs art, and not to make bourgeois art for a few and ignore the masses."*

*"Cranbrook was pretty cool. I did probably my best painting to date!"*

*"A lot of the things that I went through were temporary things. I knew when I was asked to do the piece here, at Cranbrook, that that was the situation. If I didn't want to do it, I would have said no at that point. After I did it, my first reaction when I see it is that it's one of the best drawings that I've ever done. To date. When I was finished I already missed it. I'm going to leave tomorrow and not see it again, ever. I did as much as I could to photograph it because photographs save it forever… It's really a beautiful room as far as human scale… They didn't want a Keith Haring wing in the museum, they want an ongoing exhibition space. So, in a way it's like a sacrificial thing, but it also adds to the whole energy of doing the piece."*

Haring's social activism and powerful imagery became iconic illustrations against the AIDS epidemic, which devastated the gay community, taking many of his friends, culminating with his death from the disease in 1990. I'm glad I had the opportunity to hang out with him, if only for a short time.

**Minoru Yamasaki (1912-1986), Architect,** became one of the greatest architects of the 20th century after moving to Detroit in 1945 and starting his own design firm in 1949. The One Woodward building in Detroit is a great example of his design, and was his inspiration for the World Trade Center in New York City.

*"The World Trade Center is a living symbol of man's dedication to world peace... a representation of man's belief in humanity, his need for individual dignity, his beliefs in the cooperation of men, and, through cooperation, his ability to find greatness."*

*"And a building must be like a human being. It must have a wholeness about it, something that is very important."*

*"I feel this is very important for us to have serene buildings because our civilization is chaotic as it is, you see; our whole machine age has brought about a chaos that has to be somehow counterbalanced, I think."*

Yamasaki combined his Japanese heritage with modern building design, believing that no matter the size of a building, it should embody a human scale.

**Harry Callahan (1912-1999), Photographer,** joined the Chrysler Corporation camera club in 1938.

Self-taught, Harry became friends with another great photographer, Todd Webb, also from Detroit. Although Callahan worked for many national magazines, he is known for his personal work, photographing his family.

*"I wish more people felt that photography was an adventure the same as life itself and felt that their individual feelings were worth expressing. To me, that makes photography more exciting."*

*"Experience is the best teacher of all. And for that, there are no guarantees that one will become an artist. Only the journey matters."*

*"In terms of art, the only real answer that I know of is to do it. If you don't do it, you don't know what might happen."*

*"Nearly every artist continually wants to reach the edge of nothingness – the point where you can't go any further."*

Harry loved photography, and he sparked my love for it too. He would go out every day and shoot whatever he encountered. Considered an innovator of modern photography, Harry experimented with multiple exposures, various techniques, and color film.

**Charles McGee (1924- ), Artist,** moved to Detroit when he was 10 years old. Celebrated as one of the great African-American artists of his time, he doesn't consider himself a black artist, a Detroit artist, or an American artist.

*"Learn what the artist was thinking about – I don't want to cut off my ear and that is what people talk about. Life events should not be the main feature in talking about art."*

*"I have to run as far as I can. It's like I just came out of the womb. If you stop learning – God, what is there?"*

*"The legacy I feel we leave is that our young people, regardless of their circumstances... that they can achieve if they believe it."*

His lyrical, sweeping abstract lines run counter to the gray post-industrial look of Detroit.

**Tyree Guyton (1955- ), Artist,** created a playground of art on Heidelberg Street. Despairing over the many abandoned homes nearby, Tyree began using them as the canvas for his art. Using these crumbling structures, he sought to illustrate the neglect throughout the city and to raise awareness about the plight of the neighborhoods.

*"Life itself is an art form."*

*"I strive to be a part of the solution. I see and understand how order is needed in the world and in our individual lives. My experiences have granted me knowledge of how to create art and how to see beauty in everything that exists."*

*"When you come to the Heidelberg Project, I want you to think—really think! My art is a medicine for the community. You can't heal the land until you heal the minds of the people."*

Tyree is a good friend, so it bothered me when his work, exposing the lack of attention towards the neighborhoods, was originally seen by local officials as an insult. Finally, his work has been recognized internationally and Tyree has been embraced by Detroit for his decade-long project.

**Gilda Snowden (1954-2014), Artist,** was a Cass Tech and Wayne State University graduate, and a long-time matriarch of the Detroit arts community. The Gilda

Award is given annually by the Kresge Foundation, in honor of her work, to Detroit-based artists.

*"All art is local – that's what grew you."*

*"It felt kind of strange to say I make art for money, because I make art for myself. I make choices about my paintings based on not whether it will sell."*

There was no one who represented the arts community more than Gilda. Detroit lost a treasure when she passed. Her mark will be felt for years.

**John Sinclair (1941- ), Poet,** became a provocative leader for Detroit's youth in the 1960s. Founder of the Detroit Artists Workshop, he became a contributor to *The Fifth Estate*, an anti-authoritarian magazine and possibly the oldest anarchist periodical in North America. He was sentence to ten years for passing two joints to an undercover officer, sparking a national outrage and protests. The John Sinclair Freedom Rally in 1971 was the originator of Ann Arbor's Hash Bash, an annual protest for the legalization of marijuana.

*"I was a warrior because I thought we could overthrow the government. Once I figured out that we couldn't, it seemed kind of stupid."*

*"You can do whatever you want to do; this is America. But if you're an artist you take a vow of poverty."*

*"Nobody knows anything about hippies. All of our real stories from the time period have been erased."*

John was a tremendous influence during the counterculture movement. His anti-racism, anti-capitalism, and anti war writings and activism helped define a generation. I have always admired his determination and intelligence in seeking equality and justice, and exposing the hypocrisies of our political and corporate leaders.

**Gary Grimshaw (1946-2014), Graphic Designer,** grew up with Rob Tyner and Wayne Kramer of the MC5. He began creating posters for Russ Gibb at the Grande Ballroom. Gary's work became the illustrations of a generation when Detroit was the epicenter of the rock and roll world.

*"I wanted to do posters like they were doing out in San Francisco, at the Fillmore."*

Gary went on to become the Minister of Art for John Sinclair's White Panther Party. His most memorable work was created for the 1971 John Sinclair Freedom Rally held in Ann Arbor, which included performances by John Lennon, Stevie Wonder, and Bob Seger.

**Edward Fella (1938- ), Graphic Designer,** learned graphic design at Cass Tech, graduating in 1957. He spent the next 30 years, kicking around different ad agencies and designing posters for the Detroit Focus Gallery.

*"Execution before conception. Meaning before perception."*

*"They were very controversial. A lot of the artists hated the things, but other artists welcomed them."*

Throughout his career, Ed broke most of the typical rules in typography. His work has influenced a younger generation of designers and he became the "Graphic Godfather."

**Jim Pallas (1941- ), Artist,** moved to the Cass Corridor in 1959, and throughout the 1960s and 1970s, Jim pioneered the usage of electronics in his kinetic sculptures.

*"Boredom is the failure of imagination."*

*"The enemy of art is often the janitor."*

Cass Corridor artists, including Jim, gained national acclaim as a movement, as they damn well should have.

**Ellen Phelen (1943- ), Artist,** was another of the great Cass Corridor artists of the 1960s and 1970s. After working as an assistant to Sam Wagstaff, at the Detroit Institute of Arts, Ellen, moved to New York City in 1973.

*"I started working in the context of early post-Minimalism. At the time there was this scene in Detroit, a rough, gritty Motor City junk aesthetic. It was also quite macho, lots of guys."*

Her work has developed since her days in the Corridor but you can still see the imprints of her time here.

**Mike Kelley (1954-2012), Artist,** formed the band Destroy All Monsters in 1973, with Jim Shaw, Niagara and Cary Loren. A mix of hard Detroit noise rock and performance art, DAM experimented with modified instruments, a drum box and tape loops. After graduating from the University of Michigan, Mike went on to CalArts, where he explored a variety of media, including sculpture, performance, video, and painting – which he continued to do throughout his life.

*"Basically, gift giving is like indentured slavery or something. There's no price, so you don't know how much you owe. The commodity is the emotion. What's being bought and sold is emotion."*

*"Advertising still presents an idealized notion of the family, even if it doesn't exist anymore."*

*"Paranoia is a fear that is too ludicrous to be taken seriously, but conspiracy theory has a veneer of validity, like art. You can trace it, it's based on historical information, it can be catalogued."*

Using art as commentary on American class and pop culture, Kelley became one of the greatest American artists of his time. His installations recreate earlier experiences as if he were trying to reveal or resolve events in his life.

**Jerome Ferretti (1952- ), Sculptor,** attended CCS and WSU, expanding his family's legacy as masons into a career as a sculptor. His work is in the collection of the City of Detroit and his iconic "Monumental Kitty" is another one of my favorite public art installations in Detroit.

*"Detroit has world class artists, yet, the people in Detroit are mostly working-class and would rather buy a sea-doo or ski-doo then pay for art."*

One of my best friends, Jake has been a legend in the art world, bridging the works of the Cass Corridor Movement to the younger generation of upcoming artists.

**Chris Turner (1965- ), Sculptor,** another of my close friends, grew up in Detroit and attended Cass Tech. Originally a metal worker, Chris was too independent for that career. Along with Matt Blake, Chris designed the "Millennium Bell" in Grand Circus Park.

*"Keep your stick on the ice."*

*"Stay Black."*

Every time I hang out with Chris, he tells me that when we say our goodbyes, and every time I gotta keep telling him, "I'm not Black, I'm dark red." His band, with Rob Smith, Dark Red, must've got the name from me.

**Mitch Cope (1973- ), Artist,** co-founded the Tangent Gallery and has curated many shows and at galleries around Detroit. Mitch helped form the Museum of Contemporary Art Detroit in 2007 and founded the Detroit Tree of Heaven Workshop in 2005.

*"There is a phenomenon people are referring to as 'two Detroits,' which is a privileged, mostly white Detroiter and an excluded, mostly under privileged black Detroiter within these new investments. This also shouldn't surprise people who know the history of racism in the city, but it still goes to show that we haven't learned much from the mistakes of the past."*

*"Because Detroit is THE iconic American city. From its rise, to its fall and now to its resurgence and its continued struggles, every aspect of American life is in hyper drive in Detroit –the economy, race relations, the rich, the poor, architecture, art and music – they are seen here distilled down into a range of extremes."*

*"My hope is that Detroit can retain its integrity and spirit while it also is able to grow again."*

Mitch, has spent most of his life advocating for Detroit and using the city as a canvas to illustrate the possibilities and issues which Detroit confronts.

**John Varvatos (1962- ), Fashion Designer,** grew up in Detroit and began working with Ralph Lauren and Calvin Klein. As head of design at Calvin Klein, Varvatos introduced the "boxer brief, considered by some to be one of the greatest apparel revolutions of the past century.

*"For me, growing up in Detroit, scarves meant cold weather. But I remember working in a store, and we had some silk scarves – like, wide scarves with fringe – and because I had seen the English rockers wearing skinny silk scarves, I took the scarves, cut and sewed them, and made them long – almost like a tie."*

*"Canada – they won't like me saying this, but it's really like it's a part of Michigan, that area."*

In 1999, John started his own line and credits his fashion influence from his early Detroit rock and roll days.

**Tracy Reese (1954-2012), Fashion Designer,** graduated from Cass Tech in fashion design in 1982.

After moving to New York City for school, Tracy worked at a few top fashion houses until creating her own label in 1998.

*"Every woman is not a runway model, nor should she be."*

*"You have to be the person you want to be – and start now. If you don't begin the process yourself, you're going to be waiting forever."*

*"You can make clothing as art, but I like the idea of my clothes actually being worn and being useful to women."*

In 2006, she opened her flagship store on Fifth Avenue in NYC. Michelle Obama is one her clients. Tracy is one of many from Cass Tech's class of 1982, and I know most of them, who have gone on to great success.

# ON MUSIC

*"Kick Out the Jams, Motherfuckers!"*
- MC5

Detroit *is* the Music Capital of the World! Music has always been in our soul. Beginning with Theodore Finney and his big band sound in 1857 and the birth of "Ragtime" led by Harry P. Guy, proceeding to jazz and blues legends Donald Byrd and John Lee Hooker, Detroit has always been known for an original sound. The Motown Sound was the nation's soundtrack during the 1960s and '70s. Gospel music, with Aretha Franklin, the Winans, and the Clark Sisters, is central to Detroit. The origins of punk rock and glam rock were led by such bands as the Stooges, the MC5, and Alice Cooper, while rock and roll legends Bob Seger and Ted Nugent got their start in Detroit. In the late 1980s, Derrick May and Carl Craig introduced techno to the world. Detroit music continued with the indie rock stylings of Negative Approach, the White Stripes, and Detroit Cobras, while Eminem exploded on the rap scene.

# Blues

**John Lee Hooker (1917?-2001),** originally hailed from the cotton fields of Mississippi. Like many southern blacks, he made his way to Detroit during WWII. Adrift in Detroit, the veteran bluesmen found a new home in the Hastings Street clubs where his southern blues music struck a chord. Hooker would call Detroit his home for the next 27 years, witnessing dramatic social changes, first hand.

*"I was happy in Detroit because I loved the music."*

*"Detroit was hot [in the 1940s and 1950s]. That was the place, it was nothing like it is now. After the riots [in 1967], it wasn't the same. But back then, Detroit, Michigan, was the place! I think about those times a lot."*

*"The blues tells a story. Every line of the blues has a meaning."*

*"I remember back in Detroit, I used to go to the Apex Bar every night after I got off work [at Ford]. The bartender there used to call me Boom Boom. I don't know why, but he did."*

*"I don't play a lot of fancy guitar. I don't want to play it. The kind of guitar I want to play is mean, mean licks."*

*"It's never hard to sing the blues. Everyone in the world has the blues…"*

I remember sitting with John on his front porch on Johnson Street in July 1967. We saw fire and smoke rise over our city. Right after that, he wrote "The Motor City Is Burning." Some record producer from Chicago tried to take credit for the song, but I know the truth.

**Little Sonny (1932- ),** arrived in Detroit in 1953 and began playing with John Lee Hooker and Eddie Kirkland. His skills on harmonica are unrivaled, but his stories about the early blues clubs in Detroit are legendary.

*"Detroit has always been overlooked because we had a wider variety of music… In Detroit, we took that Delta-blues sound and modified it into a more modern blues. We also had jazz, spirituals and pop; it was a whole different mix. Detroit's musical heritage blows Chicago out of the water."*

Still living on the eastside, Little Sonny has an amazing collection of harmonicas and photos of old shows. He is one of the most genuine people I know.

**Son House (1902-1988),** was born in Mississippi, but he, too, made his way to Detroit. His emotional style, coupled with his rhythmic drive, was a huge influence on Robert Johnson and Muddy Waters.

*"Ain't but one kind of blues and that consists of a male and female that's in love."*

*"Don't never follow your first mind, cause that's the one that's wrong. 'Cause the Devil beats God to you every time."*

After a stint in the Big House for killing a man while on stage, House spent his last years in Detroit.

**Johnnie Bassett (1935-2012),** moved from Florida as a child and grew up in Detroit. A session musician at Fortune Records, Johnnie also played with John Lee Hooker and Dinah Washington.

*"It was a good time to get to Detroit. It was a fun time, you know. People still left their doors unlocked and*

*stuff. Everybody was working and neighbors cared about each other."*

Acclaimed for his prolific guitar skills, Bassett became popular in his last two decades, which I thought were his most creative.

## Jazz

**Betty Carter (1929-1998),** was heavily influenced by Dizzy Gillespie early in her career. She was noted for her imaginative improvisational techniques and interpretations of melodies.

*"As far as family is concerned, it's been a lonesome trek…"*

*"You can do anything you want to do, if you know what to do."*

*"If you're sitting in that audience ready to fight me from the very beginning, I'm going to have a hard time getting to you. But if you've got a heart at all, I'm going to get it."*

An originator of scat singing, Betty performed with many of the early jazz greats including Lionel Hampton, Miles Davis, and Charlie Parker.

**Ron Carter (1937- ),** attended Cass Tech. He played with Miles Davis and Herbie Hancock in the 1960s. In fact, he's played with just about everybody and must be the most recorded jazz bassist of all times.

*"A good bassist determines the direction of any band."*

*"I am from the planet of elegance."*

Carter has since gone on to teach at CCNY and Julliard, but still comes home to play in Detroit from time to time.

**Yusef Lateef (1920-2013),** the composer and multi-instrumentalist, is considered a pioneer for his use of non-western instruments. His experimentation in Eastern music and Savoy recordings were an early influence on John Coltrane.

*"When the soul looks out of its body, it should see only beauty in its path. These are the sights we must hold in mind, in order to move to a higher place."*

*"External instruments are only extensions of the biological instrument."*

*"I started in high school with a teacher there. I also took lessons at the Conservatory of Music in Detroit.*

*Detroit was very motivating. There were a lot of local people who inspired me like Kenny Burrell, Paul Chambers, Roy Brooks, Donald Byrd, etc."*

Lateef was awarded a lifetime Jazz Master Fellowship in 2010 from the NEA, the highest honor given in jazz. I still listen to Lateef's, *Detroit: Latitude 42$^0$ 30' Longitude 83$^0$* all the time. Tracks like "Eastern Market," "Belle Isle," and "Woodward Avenue" really capture the essence of the places named in their titles.

**Kenny Burrell (1931- ),** grew up in Detroit and attended Wayne State University. Starting his career with Dizzy Gillespie, Kenny recorded at the famed Fortune Records and founded the New World Music Society with fellow Detroiters Pepper Adams, Yusef Lateef, Donald Byrd, and Elvin Jones.

*"My inspiration comes from the message Duke Ellington gave – you are unique, be yourself, put out that thing that is you, then use your work ethic and produce great music."*

*"I strive for honesty in playing what I feel."*

**Donald Byrd (1932-2013),** another of the great Cass Tech graduates, began performing with Lionel

Hampton while still in school. Graduating from WSU, Byrd took in a young Herbie Hancock, mentoring his development.

*"I was being ridiculed for going to school... But, you see, I had looked hard at the other musicians and the whole show-business scene... They were doing with jazz musicians what they usually reserved for rock 'n' roll cats: making them overnight successes, then overnight antiques."*

*"I'm creative; I'm not re-creative."*

*"It's an incredible dilemma to be an artist of color and to always be in denial about that, saying, 'I'm a choreographer first and then I'm black,' when in fact, that's not the case. I'm black first and then I'm also a choreographer."*

Byrd was a huge influence in the life of the many jazz artists with whom he played, encouraging them to continue to experiment with their music and not give up ownership of their music to the publishers.

**Marcus Belgrave (1936-2015),** began his career touring with Ray Charles. Later, he worked with

Martha Reeves, the Temptations, and the Four Tops at Motown.

*"I guess that's why they say jazz is dead but it's not dead. It's been reviving itself and reshaping itself."*

A patriarch of Detroit's jazz scene, Marcus nurtured a younger generation as he became a world-class trumpeter.

## Rhythm and Blues

**Wilson Pickett (1941-2006),** moved to Detroit from Alabama, in 1955, with his father. His singing style was influenced by the churches and streets of Detroit.

*"Soul ain't nothing but a feeling."*

*"First you harmonize, then you customize."*

Wilson bounced between quite a few record companies during his career but his greatest success was at Stax, with "In the Midnight Hour" in 1965.

**Nathaniel Mayer (1944-2008),** known as Nate and Nay-Dog, became an R&B chart success story at the age of 18 with his 1962 hit "Village of Love," a song about Detroit. Considered by many to be decades before his time, Nate disappeared from the public in 1966, but returned in 2002.

*"They'll be alright. Everybody knows they're with Nay-Dog."*

*"At the time, I thought those records were OK. Not great, just OK. Now everybody's telling me I was ahead of my time. I don't know."*

Nay-Dog was an original and stands among the most talented and energetic showmen to come out of Detroit. One of the most successful acts from underappreciated Fortune Records, Nay-Dog resurrected his career in his later years and was appreciated and rediscovered by a new generation of Detroit musicians.

**Jackie Wilson (1934-1964),** led Detroit into the R&B age. Starting out at the Raven Lounge on Chene Avenue, Jackie became a dynamic stage performer. Wilson recorded seven songs written by Berry Gordy, including "Lonely Teardrops," a song I can relate to more than I care to admit.

*"If I kiss the ugliest girl in the audience, they'll all think they can have me and keep coming back and buying my records."*

With mutual appreciation, Jackie and Elvis Presley became good friends and were considered early innovators on the stage. Called the "Black Elvis," Wilson was as much an influence for Elvis, as Elvis was for Jackie.

**Berry Gordy (1929- ),** took his profits from Pickett's success and invested in his own studio. Determined to write, produce, and discover new talent, Barry formed Motown in 1960. After a stint working at a Lincoln Mercury factory, Gordy had the idea that music could also be put on an assembly line.

*"I have this ability to find this hidden talent in people that sometimes even they didn't know they had."*

*"Every day I watched how a bare metal frame, rolling down the line would come off the other end, a spanking brand-new car. What a great idea! Maybe, I could do the same thing with my music. Create a place where a kid off the street could walk in one*

*"door, an unknown, go through a process, and come out another door, a star."*

*"Motown was about music for all people – white and black, blue and green, cops and the robbers. I was reluctant to have our music alienate anyone."*

*"I'm a songwriter, that's what I love."*

The backbone of the Motown sound was "The Funk Brothers," a collection of studio musicians, who played most of the music on all of Motown's hits. Unrecognized for decades, their crucial involvement in creating that great Motown sound is now finally gaining appreciation. Incorporating the songwriting talents of Holland-Dozier-Holland, coupled with the musical talents of the Funk Brothers, Motown became a Top 40 hit machine.

**Smokey Robinson (1940- ),** went to Northern High School and began collaborating with Berry Gordy in 1957. Signed more for his songwriting talents then his singing, Smokey is credited with many of Motown's early hits.

*"One thing I can say about the Motown acts is that we were a family. That's not a myth."*

*"I don't ever balk at being considered a Motown person, because Motown is the greatest musical event that ever happened in the history of music."*

*"That's because we did not set out to make black music. We set out to make quality music that everyone could enjoy and listen to."*

Although his early success was in songwriting, Smokey became one of Motown's biggest stars. I believe Motown would've never achieved the heights of success it did without Smokey's talents as a producer and writer.

**Diana Ross (1944- ),** grew up blocks from Smokey and graduated from Cass Tech. As a member of the Supremes, Diana struggled to find a hit song. Finally, in 1964, the song "Where Did Our Love Go" was the first of twelve number one hits, a record.

*"I lived on the north side of Detroit. Right down the street from me there was a young man by the name of Smokey Robinson. I was very proud to live down the street from him because he was our only celebrity in town. He was singing with the Miracles."*

*"You can't just sit there and wait for people to give*

*you that golden dream. You've got to get out there and make it happen for yourself."*

*"Most people are so hard to please that if they met God, they'd probably say yes, she's great, but…"*

*"It takes a long time to get to be a diva. I mean, you gotta work at it."*

Considered Berry's muse, Diana became one of Motown's most famous stars. The Queen of Divas, Ross went on to a successful solo career.

**Stevie Wonder (1950- ),** signed with Motown at the age of 11. One of the most prolific songwriters of the past century, Stevie became one of Motown's greatest stars.

*"Music, at its essence, is what gives us memories. And the longer a song has existed in our lives, the more memories we have of it."*

*"Let us come together before we're annihilated."*

*"What I'm not confused about is the world needing much more love, no hate, no prejudice, no bigotry and more unity, peace and understanding. Period."*

*"If you don't ask, you don't get."*

Stevie and I hit it off when I first met him. Due to his blindness, Stevie didn't see me as a red gnome or devilish character. He saw me as an equal, just like everyone else.

**Marvin Gaye (1939-1984),** became an essential part of Motown during the 1960s, pumping out hit after hit. His groundbreaking hit, "What's Going On?" broke the long-standing rule against political songs at Motown and became one of their biggest hits.

*"If you cannot find peace within yourself, you will never find it anywhere else."*

*"I hope to refine music, study it, try to find some area that I can unlock. I don't quite know how to explain it but it's there. These can't be the only notes in the world, there's got to be other notes some place, in some dimension, between the cracks on the piano keys."*

*"Music, not sex, got me aroused."*

*"Detroit turned out to be heaven, but it also turned out to be hell."*

If there is one person who epitomizes R&B, it is Marvin. His soulful voice and gospel background created the voice that every other singer has tried to imitate.

**Gladys Knight (1944- ),** is known as the "Empress of Soul." Knight, accompanied by her brother and cousins, the Pips, stormed the charts in the early '70s.

*"If all I do in my life is soothe someone's spirit with a song, then let me do that and I'm happy."*

*"Soul is just that inner spirit. I use that inner spirit for whatever it is I do."*

Gladys, with her amazing voice, was one of the last great Motown stars who called Detroit home.

**George Clinton (1941- ),** began his musical career as a songwriter for Motown. George went on to develop funk music through his bands Parliament and Funkadelic. Later in his career, many of his songs were sampled by younger artists. Clinton remarked:

*"Sure, sample my stuff… Ain't a better time to get paid than when you're my age. You know what to do with money. You don't buy as much pussy or drugs with it – you just buy some."*

A prolific producer and performer, Clinton brought over the top orchestrations, wardrobe, and production to his stage shows. I like to think he picked up a few style tips from yours truly.

**Ray Parker Jr. (1954- ),** attended Cass Tech and graduated from Northwestern High School. As a teenager, Ray co-wrote songs with Marvin Gaye. Parker went on to perform with most of the 1970s R&B stars.

*"A lot of it starts with playing instruments and working with other people. Some of the new generation is doing it on computers and they don't have a clue as to how to play anything. That's probably one of the problems. They don't know how to make the melody, go through the chord changes. They're not starting from that same school of thought."*

Pursuing a solo career, Ray went on to have several hits and was a pioneer in producing music videos for black audiences.

**Anita Baker (1958- ),** was abandoned by her mother at two and was raised by a foster family. At 12, her foster parents died and she was raised by her foster sister and began playing in local nightclubs at the age of 16.

*"I don't think being black has held me back at all. Being black makes you strong."*

*"My father worked on assembly lines in Detroit while I was growing up. Every day, I watched him do what he needed to do to support the family. But he told me, 'Life is short. Do what you want to do.'"*

Anita found success with her first LP in 1983.

## Gospel

**Della Reese (1931- ),** began singing in her Black Bottom church at the age of six. While attending Cass Tech, at 13, she was discovered by and toured with Mahalia Jackson.

*"You see, I was born in the slums, that was before the ghetto. The ghetto was kind of refined; the slums was right there on the ground."*

*"If you're not getting the things you want, need or desire, it's because you have not accepted that you can have them."*

*"I don't see how I possibly could have come from where I entered the planet to where I am now if there had not been angels along the way."*

Della was a successful gospel and jazz singer when she transitioned to TV, becoming the first black guest host of *The Tonight Show*, in 1970, hosting her own TV show, and starring on others. Folks who prejudge me because of my appearance might not believe I appreciate gospel music, but I do – and have ever since I first heard Della sing.

**Aretha Franklin (1942- ),** "The Queen of Soul", started out as a child singer at her father's church, New Bethel Baptist Church. Many great singers and celebrities would visit the Franklin home, exposing Aretha to the world of gospel music.

*"Be your own artist, and always be confident in what you're doing. If you're not going to be confident, you might as well not be doing it."*

*"Music does a lot of things for a lot of people. It's transporting, for sure. It can take you right back, years back, to the very moment certain things happened in your life. It's uplifting, it's encouraging, it's strengthening."*

*"We all require and want respect, man or woman, black or white. It's our basic human right."*

*"Soul is a constant. It's cultural. It's always going to be there, in different flavors and degrees."*

Though she started in gospel music, Aretha went on to become the number-one pop and R&B diva in the world.

The Winans are a family of great gospel singers from Prefecting Church on Detroit's eastside. Discovered by Andrae Crouch and James Cleveland, the many Winan siblings have gone on to solo careers.

**BeBe Winans (1942- ),** spells out what could be my own personal philosophy:

*"Love is so unconditional; love liberates; love is the reason why I do what I do, and so I think it is the greatest gift we have."*

**Marvin Winans (1958- ),** gets to the heart of the matter when it comes to gospel:

*"Gospel will never go away because it reaches everyone in a space that longs to hear those things."*

**CeCe Winans (1964- ),** says it best, about both gratitude and equality:

*"When the song is over, the mikes turned off, the lights dimmed, all the glitter and glamour shed, and I am left alone with my own thoughts, free to contemplate the paths that led me to where I am today, I pause to give thanks."*

*"The rich people are doing well but regular people suffer. We'll all be better off when we realize that we're part of one big family."*

Recognized as the "First Family of Gospel," the Winans continue to record with their church choir and tour the world.

**The Clark Sisters,** another gospel super-group, featuring the daughters of Mattie Moss Clark – Jacky, Elbernita, Dorinda and Karen – are pioneers of contemporary gospel.

**Karen Clark Sheard (1960- ),** gets to a truth that might apply as much to Detroit music generally as to gospel specifically:

*"I would like to appeal to different audiences – to*

*reach the world and a lot of young people who don't go to church."*

The Clark Sisters are known the world over and are credited with bringing gospel music to the mainstream.

## Pop

**Sonny Bono (1935-1998),** was born in Detroit and named after his father, Santo. "Sonny" got his nickname from his mother and it stuck. Starting out as a songwriter, Sonny worked as a "gofer" for Phil Spector. Teamed with his wife, Sonny and Cher achieved commercial success as singers.

*"People have said to me, you can't write songs. You can't play an instrument. But I've got 10 gold records."*

*"What is qualified? What have I been qualified for in my life? I haven't been qualified to be a mayor. I'm not qualified to be a songwriter. I'm not qualified to be a TV producer. I'm not qualified to be a successful businessman. And so, I don't know what qualified means."*

More of a B actor, Sonny's music success lasted only as long as his marriage to Cher. He eventually became a politician, but, personally, I preferred him as a singer.

**Casey Kasem (1932-2014), Disk Jockey,** a.k.a. Kemal Kasem, went to Northwestern High School and Wayne State University. In 1970, Kasem began the hit radio show, *American Top 40*.

*"I started radio in 1950 on the Lone Ranger radio program, a dramatic show that emanated from Detroit when I was 18 years old and just beginning college. I did that for a couple of years."*

*"If the beat gets to the audience, and the message touches them, you've got a hit."*

*"Keep your feet on the ground and keep reaching for stars."*

Casey also found fame as the voice for Shaggy in the popular kid's cartoons, *Scooby Doo*.

**Michael Jackson (1958-2009),** started out as the child star singer with the Jackson 5 on Motown Records. The "King of Pop," Jackson wrote and produced some of the greatest songs of the 70s and '80s, and kept producing until his unfortunate overdose.

*"I'm happy to be alive, I'm happy to be who I am."*

*"And I remember going to the record studio and there was a park across the street and I'd see all the children playing and I would cry because it would make me sad that I would have to work instead."*

Michael was an awesome singer. I remember when he first came to Motown as a shy six-year-old. Despite his upbringing amongst the many Motown R&B stars, he never outgrew his shyness.

**Madonna Ciccone (1958- ),** referred to by some as the "Queen of Pop," was born in suburban Detroit. Dropping out of the University of Michigan's Dance program, she made her way to NYC and pop music history.

*"Things were a lot simpler in Detroit. I didn't care about anything but boyfriends."*

*"Sometimes you have to be a bitch to get things done."*

*"I became an overachiever to get approval from the world."*

Understanding the trends of the times, Madonna has remade herself throughout her career, becoming one of the most popular pop stars in the world.

**Aaliyah (1979-2001),** performed at age10 with Gladys Knight and was signed to her first record deal at age 12. R. Kelly produced her first album when she was 14. She graduated from the Detroit High School for the Fine and Performing Arts.

*"I stay true to myself and my style, and I am always pushing myself to be aware of that and be original."*

*"It's hard to say what I want my legacy to be when I'm long gone."*

*"I want people to remember me as a full-on entertainer and a good person."*

Her popularity spiked with her debut in the film *Romeo Must Die*. After her untimely death, her music has continued to sell, earning her the nickname the "Princess of R&B."

## Rock and Roll

**Bill Haley (1925-1981),** is from Highland Park and formed Bill Haley & the Comets after his family moved to Pennsylvania during the Depression. One of the first popular acts in rock, Bill was one of the first rockabilly artists.

*"Rock 'n' roll is just entertainment, and the kids who like to identify their youthful high spirits with a solid beat are thus possibly avoiding other pursuits that could be harmful to them."*

*"The road can be hard on a kid if he's not careful."*

*"I sat down one night and wrote the line rock, rock, rock everybody."*

Bill was an innovator of the new rock and roll sound, selling over 25 million records.

**Mitch Ryder (1945- ),** known to family as William Levise, Jr., grew up in Hamtramck. His band Mitch Ryder and the Detroit Wheels set the stage for most of the Detroit rock and roll that followed him.

*"I can't be the judge of my own career. I'm not going to claim to be anything. Other people talk and say, 'He was a big inspiration to me,' and this and that, but it's really for other people to judge. All I know is I did the best I could with what I had... and it turned out to be all right."*

*"When I look back on it now, it was kind of like a waste of time more than it was fun. What we needed*

*to be doing was constantly creating and practicing 24 hours a day. If you're going to sacrifice a family to be out there making music, then you need to pay a penance for it and that would be to be true to your art form. And we weren't. We were just out partying, so I thought, 'Wow, what a wasted couple of decades that was.'"*

*"To start the band 'Detroit,' I think somebody just opened the prison doors. You can tell the energy was there on the music, but the group frightened people."*

*"Detroit had become like One Flew over the Cuckoo's Nest."*

A mentor to Bob Seger, Bruce Springsteen, John Mellencamp and Ted Nugent, Mitch made music built to last and his influence lives on.

**John Sinclair (1941- ),** became spiritual leader and manager of the famed MC5, and in 1968 co-founded the White Panther Party, a leftist, anti-racist compliment to the Black Panther Party.

*"The MC5 was truly a wondrous thing to behold, and above and beyond everything else was the power and beauty of an MC5 performance."*

*"Holding nothing back, the 5 pounded and pulsated with unbelievable energy and incredible stagecraft."*

*"The band's reckless advocacy of recreational drug use and its all-out, gob-of-spit-in-the-face-of-god-for-art defiance of authority and social convention likewise inspired the punk rock movement…"*

*"The Amboy Dukes were great guys, but Ted Nugent – how could you trust a guy that didn't get high?"*

Detroit was a wondrous place in the late 1960s, and Sinclair was a leader for a new generation. He believed in free thought and progressive arts and music. I believe John's influence and prestige effected the following generation of Detroit radicals.

**MC5 (1964-1972),** was the quintessential Detroit rock and roll band in the 1960s and early '70s. Although their time was short, their light burned brightest, influencing generations of musicians and movements. As house band at the famed Grande Ballroom, the MC5 led a generation into the world of drugs, politics, and revolution. It was my idea for them to cover my man John Lee Hooker's "Motor City Is Burning."

**Rob Tyner (1944-1991),** was born Robert Derminer and adopted the last name by which he became known as the lead singer of the MC5 to honor jazz pianist McCoy Tyner. He grew up in Lincoln Park. A political leftist, much like Sinclair, Tyner led the MC5 into the '60s political revolution.

*"This is the night we've been working for all our lives, when the MC5 will unleash sonic fury and devastate the cosmos with mega bursts of thunder."*

*"We were punk before punk. We were New Wave before New Wave. We were Metal before Metal."*

**Wayne Kramer (1948- ),** was a guitarist for the MC5 and is still creating and producing music. His jail troubles were noted in a 1977 Clash song, "Jail Guitar Doors."

*"The MC5 was hard chargin' and all out. There were no reservations. The MC5 was visceral – all sweat and muscle and the whole concept of high energy. It's a real thing… It's a way of life and a way to play music."*

*"If you put this in the context of Detroit in '64 or '65, the economy was booming. Everybody had jobs and*

*there was a whole nightclub culture where bands could work."*

*"Aesthetically, we were enormously successful. Economically... there was no success. It was all about music of the future and unfortunately it was a band that didn't have any future."*

The MC5 never made it commercially outside Detroit, but their hard driving rock and roll, theatrics, and politics have left a lasting legacy.

**The Stooges (1967-1974),** were formed in Ann Arbor when Iggy met the Asheton brothers, Ron and Scott. Playing around Detroit, and billed as the "Psychedelic Stooges" by the Grande Ballroom, they signed to Elektra in 1968.

**Iggy Pop (1947- ),** was born in Muskegon as James Osterberg, Jr., and grew up in Ypsilanti and Ann Arbor. After seeing an MC5 show in Ann Arbor, James changed his name to Iggy Pop.

*"I became Iggy because I had a sadistic boss at a record store. I'd been in a band called the Iguanas. And when this boss wanted to embarrass and demean me, he'd say, 'Iggy, get me a coffee, light.'"*

*"Music is life, and life is not a business."*

*"They say that death kills you, but death doesn't kill you. Boredom and indifference kill you."*

*"I like music that's more offensive. I like it to sound like nails on a blackboard, get me wild."*

*"I'm not ashamed to dress 'like a woman' because I don't think it's shameful to be a woman."*

One of the hardest charging bands in rock and roll, the Stooges, with Iggy's on-stage antics and Ron Asheton's guitar power chords, led to the punk rock era. Iggy, "The Godfather of Punk Rock," went on to a successful solo career.

**Alice Cooper (1948- ),** was born in Detroit as Vincent Furnier but moved to Phoenix, Arizona, as a teenager for his health. After signing with Frank Zappa, and failing to connect with West Coast audiences, Cooper returned to Detroit, where he was received as one of our own. Competing on stage with the MC5, the Stooges, and Ted Nugent, Alice began creating his famed theatrical stage persona.

*"It was a hard-drug city, but it was the best Rock and Roll city ever."*

*"The late sixties and early seventies were kind of a breeding ground for exciting new sounds because easy listening and folk were kind of taking over the airwaves. I think it was a natural next step to take that blissful, easy-going sound and strangle the life out of it."*

*"I appreciate an audience that reacts to the music, even if they jump on stage and try to beat us up, I think that's a fantastic reaction. I think that they're really hearing something then."*

*"I always tell people, 'Everything you've heard about Alice Cooper, you can believe maybe 40 percent of it. Everything you've ever heard about Keith Moon is true – and you've only heard 10 percent of it.'"*

*"Just because I cut the heads off dolls doesn't mean I hate babies, I just hate dolls."*

*"L.A. just didn't get it, they were all on the wrong drug for us. They were on acid and we were basically drinking beer. We fit much more in Detroit than we did anywhere else."*

As Detroit audiences embraced his androgynous stage performances, the "Godfather of Shock Rock" and the band found greater confidence creating music, resulting in multiple hits and the anthem "Schools Out."

**Bob Seger (1945- ),** was born in Detroit and moved to Ann Arbor at age five. At 16, Bob started playing around town, going from one band to another, until forming the Bob Seger System in 1966. Pursued by Motown, Seger signed with Capitol for more money in 1968. In 1974, he formed the Silver Bullet Band.

*"By being in Detroit, I can keep things in perspective… and where people put me in my place. Everybody there treats me just like a guy and not a rock star."*

*"Mediocrity's easy, the good things take time, the great need commitment."*

*"When you're in a relationship, you're always surrounded by a ring of circumstances… joined together by a wedding ring, or in a boxing ring."*

*"It took me a long time to learn how to write a good song."*

*"When you have kids, you start thinking about their future and you forget about yours."*

Although Seger found instant success in Detroit, it took years for him to break out nationally. Finally recognized as one of the rock's great song writers, Bob continues to stay close to home.

**Glenn Frey (1948-2016),** grew up outside Detroit in Royal Oak. Glenn befriended Bob Seger in 1967 and wanted to join Seger's band. Glenn's mother stopped him because she found out they were smoking pot together. Moving to L.A. in 1970, Frey met Don Henley and soon became a member of the Eagles.

*"We set out to become a band for our time. But sometimes if you do a good-enough job, you become a band for all time."*

*"Except for a few guitar chords, everything I've learned in my life that is of any value I've learned from women."*

*"People don't run out of dreams – people just run out of time."*

*"Detroit... where 'mother' is half a word."*

Not a bad music career – despite Mom's interference.

**Ted Nugent (1948- ),** is from Redford, just outside Detroit. He started performing at age ten and joined the Amboy Dukes in Chicago in 1964. Relocating to Detroit, Ted replaced most of the Chicago bandmates with Detroiters. Firmly anti-drug and alcohol, Nugent was an anomaly in the Detroit scene. The Dukes big hit, "Journey to the Center of the Mind," from 1968, became a LSD drug anthem.

*"When I got back and watched the MC5, I was not quite prepared for that."*

*"I was gonna pursue my musical dream with a vengeance, and God help anybody who got in my way."*

*"I brought every Detroit spirit, every Detroit attitude and just gave the finger to Chicago."*

*"I am the Great White Buffalo and I play an American-made Gibson guitar that can blow your head clean off at 100 paces."*

*"I'm so much fun. Every kid wishes I was their grandpa! I'm the Motor City Madgramps."*

Although Ted has gone alt-right crazy, he wasn't always that way. In 1968, Ted played with other artists including Jimi Hendrix and Buddy Guy in NYC to honor Martin Luther King Jr., the day after his assassination.

**Russ Gibb (1931- ),** was a DJ on WKNR in Detroit when he began promoting the famed Grande Ballroom in 1966. The Grande became the rock venue for national touring acts and introduced some of Detroit's greats, including the MC5, Alice Cooper, Ted Nugent, Bob Seger, and the Stooges. The Who performed *Tommy* for the first time in the United States at the Grande.

*"It really started as a matter of convenience for the English bands. Once they played the Grande and saw the sound was great, they spread the word. And once word got out in England that there was a great place where the people were cool, and the sound was cool and the city was cool, the Grande became a legend."*

*"Iggy did invent the stage dive."*

*"I saw them [Negative Approach] and I said, 'Wow, this is interesting.' They're doing things that the MC5 were doing. This is 15 years later."*

"Uncle" Russ to those who knew him, Gibbs with Touch and Go Records started the Graystone, featuring indie and punk rock in the 1980s.

**Lester Bangs (1948-1982),** was a journalist and, in 1971, became editor for *Creem* magazine, founded in Detroit, in 1969. Called "America's greatest rock critic," Bangs was acerbic and disdainful of celebrity.

*"Detroit is rock's only hope."*

*"Music, you know, true music not just rock 'n' roll, chooses you."*

*"The first mistake of art is to assume that it's serious."*

*"Rock 'n' roll is an attitude, it's not a musical form of a strict sort. It's a way of doing things, of approaching things. Writing can be rock 'n' roll, or a movie can be rock 'n' roll. It's a way of living your life."*

Lester loved Detroit, its rock fans, and the bands that came out of here. Bangs made *Creem* a national magazine rivaling *Rolling Stone*.

**Dave Marsh (1950- ),** was born in Waterford, outside Detroit. Dave was a close friend of Lester Bangs and a rock critic and editor at *Creem*.

*"Sometimes the tenderest thing you can do for a person is smash them right in the teeth!"*

*"I argue with lots of things, but I do not argue with my ears."*

While at *Creem*, Marsh began categorizing early garage bands like the MC5 and the Stooges, as "punk rock," defining the term.

**Sixto Rodriguez (1942- ),** was named "Sixto" because he was the sixth child of Mexican immigrants. After he wrote and recorded two albums in the early 1970s, critics compared him to Bob Dylan, but sales in the United States were poor. Dropped from his label, Sixto quit music in 1976 and raised a family. During the 1980s, South Africa was under apartheid, and most labels refused to sell records there. In 1997, his daughter discovered a website searching for his whereabouts. Unknown to the rest of the world, in South Africa, his songs had become anti-apartheid anthems.

*"I'm not old – I'm ancient. But there's only one age: either you're alive or you're not."*

*"Hate is too strong of an emotion to waste on someone you don't like."*

Playing to sold-out shows in South Africa in 1998,

Sixto became a worldwide sensation. The movie *Searching for Sugarman* recalls the events leading up to his rediscovery. Every now and again, you'll find me with Jerome Ferretti and Sixto sharing stories and a drink at the Old Miami.

**Death (1971-1976),** was formed in 1971 by brothers Bobby, David and Dannis Hackney. Influenced by the Who and Alice Cooper, the trio went on to record only seven songs at United Sound Systems recording studio in Detroit. As an all-black punk rock band during the '70s, they didn't have a chance.

*"The concept was spinning death from the negative to the positive. It was a hard sell."*

Death was ahead of their time. Rediscovered in 2007, the band is finally being recognized for their songs. The 2012 documentary *A Band Called Death* reveals their struggles getting into the music industry.

**Don Was (1952- ), Was (Not Was),** or Don Faganson, grew up in Detroit's suburbs and spent his early days in the rock scene until forming Was (Not Was) with his childhood friend, David Weiss, a.k.a. David Was. He has since become a prolific producer.

*"I did drop out of school."*

*"You know all I wanted out of life was to not have to go to work, get by playing music."*

With an amalgam of styles performed by a collection of studio and guest musicians, Was (Not Was) debuted their first album in 1981. Every year, Don returns to Detroit for the Concert of Colors series of free shows, which I always attend.

**Patti Smith (1946- ),** the brilliant poet, musician, and memoirist, wasn't born in the Detroit area, of course, but she did live in it for a time after she married Fred "Sonic" Smith, who had been one of the MC5's guitarists before forming his own band.

*"It was March 9, 1976, and we met in front of the radiator at that hot dog place, Lafayette Coney Island, in Detroit. The Sonic Rendezvous Band was opening for us, but I didn't know anything about him. Lenny [Kaye] introduced me to this guy. I heard that his name was Smith, and my name is Smith. We just looked at each other and I was completely taken by him. I had no idea who he was or anything about him until afterwards when Lenny told me. Lenny introduced him and said, 'He's one of the great guitar*

*players.' I said, 'Perhaps you'll want to play with us tonight.' And he said, 'Maybe so.' Then he left and I asked Lenny if he was really good, and Lenny said, 'the best.' So, I was playing with him that night, and I had a lot of bravado in those days. I didn't have respect for anybody. But I totally submitted to his reign. He came on the stage and started playing, and after a while I just set my guitar down and let it feedback. I just let him take over because I felt I had met my match, that I had met the better man."*

Fred "Sonic" Smith and Patty, played music and house together until Fred's untimely death. They have two incredibly talented children, Jackson and Jesse, both good friends.

**John Bandajek, Mitch Ryder and the Detroit Wheels, Detroit, The Rockets,** began as drummer for Mitch Ryder and the Detroit Wheels when he was just 16, and also played in the band called Detroit. Dave Marsh called him an "unknown genius" for his drum break on "Devil With a Blue Dress On."

*"What finally happened with 'Detroit,' is that the band became bikers. It was like we weren't musician; we were an outlaw biker club."*

Johnny "Bee" formed the Rockets in 1972. His career has spanned the glory days of 1960s Detroit rock and roll to today.

**Mike Skill, The Romantics,** joined the Romantics in 1977, just as Detroit rock and roll was moving towards the New Wave and punk scenes. Red leather suits became the band's trademark, much to my objections.

*"The natural progression was to do the leather because, well, the Dolls used to do it."*

One of many talented bands during this period, the Romantics were the only band signed by a major label.

**Jerry Vile, The Boners**, or Jerry Peterson, is a provocateur. His band, the Boners, became known for their outrageous costumes and dirty lyrics. Publisher of the satiric magazines *White Noise* and *Orbit*, Jerry is also a visual artist. Jerry coined a certain phrase decades before Vegas did:

*"What happens in Detroit, stays in Detroit."*

*"You'd think bikers would love punk rock, but they don't. Bikers like gentle music."*

*"I also had a band, the Boners, that I started. Then I had even more excuses to be an asshole."*

*"The whole Detroit punk thing – nobody made it, and there are a lot of reasons. The record covers looked like shit."*

Creator of the pornographic art party "The Dirty Show," Vile has spent his life provoking audiences with his acerbic talents.

**John Brannon (1961- ), Negative Approach, Laughing Hyenas, Easy Action,** is the "Godfather of Detroit Punk Rock," although he would scoff at me for such a title. His band Negative Approach, along with a few others during this time, rejected the corporate music scene as it was expanding into arena shows, with costumes and pretentious songs. In 1980, a whole new scene for raw rock and roll developed at the Freezer, a small warehouse in Detroit. Bands like the Necros, the Meatmen, the Fix, and L-Seven led the way for a young disaffected audience.

*"Cream was like the bible to me growing up."*

*"You want to talk about punk rock. I'm gonna go Stooges, MC5, real Detroit rock, Alice Cooper."*

*"Okay, we're bored, we live in Detroit, we're going to create nothing out of nothing."*

*"We were writing the soul music of the suburbs, and the Freezer was perfect."*

*"We always attracted the nuts, for sure, then they'd end up on tour with us."*

Negative Approach only lasted two years, until it reformed a decade ago with a new fan base. John formed another great band, the Laughing Hyenas with Larissa, and later, Easy Action.

**Tesco Vee, The Meatmen,** is another of the great leaders of Detroit punk rock. With his band the Meatmen, Tesco was the most outrageous frontman in all of rock music.

*"Mom warned me about gay guys, but she didn't warn me about girls in the men's room. What do I do know? I just hid my penis and peed."*

*"You went to see The Romantics because all the hot girls would go."*

*"We had some really good bands and the world needed to see them."*

*"Leaving a legacy wasn't really the mark I was shooting for. I'd like to think we just left a big nasty skid mark in the underpants of punk."*

Starting the fanzine and then the label Touch and Go, he connected with small pockets of agitated youth in different cities, ultimately bringing American punk rock to the nation.

**Corey Rusk, The Necros,** played a couple years with the Necros until taking over Touch and Go Records from Tesco Vee. Touch and Go Records became the home to many of the great Midwest punk rock bands during the 1980s.

*"It was such a huge time for music. At least to us."*

*"Touch and Go was doing pretty well. We were working with the Butthole Surfers, and Big Black, and Killdozer."*

*"1981 was the year that MTV started... but it was just this bizarre upstart concept in 1981... for Russ [Gibb] to see that the future of music was in music video… and to say 'I want the kids in my class to have this experience, because this will prepare them for what is gonna be the future.'"*

Joining with Uncle Russ, from the famed Grande Ballroom, Corey opened the Graystone Ballroom in Touch and Go's HQ, hosting shows, and promoting bands.

**Jimmy Doom, Almighty Lumberjacks of Death,** and I have been friends since before he can remember. His band, the Almighty Lumber Jacks of Death, carried on the scorching punk rock that grew out of Detroit from 1987 to 1991.

*"In Detroit in our era (late 80's) bands would come here with a lot of trepidation from the reputation the press gave the city. We'd be like 'hang with us dude, we won't let anything happen to you... for a couple free t-shirts.'"*

*"Steve's Place was like a scale model of Detroit. Gritty, full of freaks but super friendly."*

At the time, St. Andrew's Hall was the venue for most great shows. Next door was the beloved Steve's Place, a dive bar run by the two kindest and most generous people in Detroit, Steve and Sophie.

**Danny Kroha, The Gories, Rocket 455, The Demolition Dollrods,** met Mick Collins, of the Dirtbombs, in the mid '80s. Deciding that even they could start a band, they formed the Gories, one of the first Detroit garage bands.

*"We were hanging out in my bedroom, listening to records, and Mick was like, 'Man, these songs have only three chords in them.' He goes, 'We can play this stuff.' I'm like, 'Well, let's do it! We should do it then!'"*

One of the Gories' first shows was part of Rob Tyner's Community Concert Series.

*"To us Rob was just some bloated old hippie playing songs about Vietnam vets on an electric autoharp. We were stupid young punks. We didn't have the foresight to realize that a Detroit music legend was giving our crappy little band a chance to play onstage at a time in our 'career' when no one in Detroit would touch us with Don Rickle's dick. I wish I could thank you now, Mr. Tyner."*

*"I met Jack [White] hanging out at the Gold Dollar... He looked up to me so much that I didn't even notice that he was, like, this much taller than me."*

*"Meg, I heard you and Jack broke up. Keep the White Stripes going. You've got something good going on."*

Danny and Mick went on to start other influential bands, including the Demolition Doll Rods, Rocket 455, and the Dirtbombs.

**Rachel Nagy, Detroit Cobras,** used to hang out in the basement where the Detroit Cobras would practice, as I sometimes did myself. Unsatisfied with the singers they auditioned, they asked Rachel to try it out. Since 1994, she and Mary Ramirez have been the only consistent members. Known for their great cover songs, the Cobras first found success in the UK.

*"They were trying to find singers and nothing was working out. I was always there, watching The Simpsons, and drinking beer and passing out. Finally, they got me drunk enough that I could get up and sing."*

*"So Kevin Monroe kicks me out... He had a bunch of his mom's antique sofas and stuff in there. I bought five 40's and I peed on everything. I peed on every sofa, corner, everything – everything I could pee on, I peed on."*

*"Jack White is the only person in the whole scene that I'm glad he has made it. He is ambitious, he's clever, and he lifted everybody up in Detroit."*

*"Let's face it: the Stooges, the MC5, Motown – that's the fucking shit. This where it all comes from."*

Over the years, almost anyone in Detroit rock and roll has played for the Cobras. It has been a launching pad to dozens of musicians while the girls just keep on rocking.

**Tommy Potter, Bantam Rooster, Dirtbombs, The Detroit City Council,** came to Detroit from mid-Michigan. His band, Bantam Rooster, was one of the first "garage bands" to begin recording and touring.

*"In Detroit back then, we all enjoyed the luxury of not having to give a fuck. In fact, the less of a fuck you gave... the better off you were."*

*"You could drive as fast as you wanted to in Detroit... It was a drunken rocker's paradise, and the only fee was having your car broken into every couple months..."*

On Danny Kroha wearing women's clothes on stage, when someone questioned his sexuality-

*"That dude gets more fucking ass then a toilet seat."*

I met Tommy when he asked me to manage his band, The Detroit City Council. During this time, the practice space was shared by so many great bands, Ko and the Knockouts, The Sights, The Blackman, I could go on and on. There was a feeling of true camaraderie amongst the musicians.

**Jack White (1975- ), The White Stripes, The Go,** was born Jack Gillis, and attended Cass Technical High School. He used to read poetry around town and met Meg at one of his shows. Jack started out playing drums with Goober and the Peas, a cow-punk band, and then played guitar for The Go before moving on to the White Stripes with Meg, whom he married.

*"I had little to no interest in anything but the music and the friendships, the family of it."*

*"Mick Collins should be bigger; he's just brilliant... and Brendan Benson too."*

*"The Gories, that was royalty to Detroit, but this is a sub-sub-genre of rock and roll."*

*"It was something I'd always wanted to do, just be a guitar player in a band. And then there was the gang mentality of it. As a drummer, you almost sometimes don't feel like you're part of the gang..."*

*"It made me, even more so, say we have this burning, volcanic scene going on… if it happened in San Diego or Chicago, it would have gotten picked up and maybe ruined, and so it was a beautiful thing about it too."*

*"It was just baby steps and learning. It wasn't my scene."*

*"Meg loves peppermints, and we were going to call ourselves The Peppermints. But since our last name was White, we decided to call it 'The White Stripes.'"*

*"I still feel we've never topped our first album. It's the most raw, the most powerful, and the most Detroit-sounding record we've made."*

On the last White Stripes show before he and Meg divorced, Jack recalled:

*"There was a moment she wasn't interested anymore for sure. We had one gig booked left…all of our friends came, and everybody sang along with the songs, it was quite shocking. It was very unlike all those people."*

*"So it was a beautiful moment… that it affected Meg enough to keep her in the band."*

Jack went on to record alongside fellow Detroiter Brendan Benson, an old roommate, with the Ranconteurs. He moved to Nashville, where he began producing and started Third Man Records. Opening a Third Man outpost in Detroit, with a record plant, Third Man offers vinyl pressings of new and old hits.

**Kid Rock (1971- ),** or Robert Ritchie, was born in Romeo, a small town north of Detroit. Bob joined a rap group called "The Beast Crew" with one of my good friends, Danny Harris, or "The Blackman," at age 15. A master at mixing rock, rap, and country, Kid has sustained his star stature by adapting his music before audiences knew they wanted a change.

*"I was the little white kid who rocked the turntables."*

*"I do not believe that artists or actors and people should be out there like voicing their full-blown opinions on politics because, let's face it, at the end of the day, I'm not that smart of a guy."*

*"Everything I've done in my career has started in and around Detroit, you know, the metro area and Michigan."*

*"Many of my lyrics are about having sex with prostitutes."*

*"If I was president of the good old U.S.A., I'd turn the churches into strip clubs and watch the whole world pray."*

*"Getting married is the most fun you can have in life. Being married sucks."*

*"The best formula for revenge is success."*

*"Detroit: Cars and rock 'n' roll. Not a bad combo."*

*"I'm from Michigan and was raised in and around Detroit where it is you get respect and you give respect. That is how I feel."*

*"Go where you're celebrated, not tolerated. I'm celebrated in Detroit."*

*"I'm in awe of people like Jerry Lee Lewis and Little Richard; they're great musicians and people. But I'm most star struck by people in the small town where I live. Especially single dads, like me, who are working five times as hard to raise their kids."*

*"I see the people in Detroit… they're very proud to be from there and they really want to see change and they really want to see good things happen."*

Always crediting Detroit for his success, Kid Rock is beloved here, his hometown. I just hope he remembers what he once said about politics…

**Detroit Audiences** are considered the greatest rock and roll audiences in the world. So many artists got their start in Detroit or wrote songs in honor of the city that embraced them before other cities recognized their talents. **Kiss** first found success in Detroit. The band wrote their classic **"Detroit Rock City"** in tribute. Other testimonials came from the **J. Geils Band**, with **"Detroit Breakdown,"** and from **David Bowie** with **"Panic in Detroit."** And then there is **Journey's "Don't Stop Believin,'"** which mentions "South Detroit" – wherever that is...

## Hip-Hop and Rap

**Eminem (1972- ),** or Marshall Mathers, is the best-selling artist of the 2000s. Attending the famed Hip Hop Shop on West 7 Mile Road, Eminem worked on his rap and writing skills, earning respect from the mostly black audiences.

*"The truth is you don't know what is going to happen tomorrow. Life is a crazy ride, and nothing is guaranteed."*

*"I say what I want to say and do what I want to do. There's no in between. People will either love you for it or hate you for it."*

*"Trust is hard to come by. That's why my circle is small and tight. I'm kind of funny about making new friends."*

*"Hip-hop is ever changing but you'll always have the pack. And you'll always have those people who are separated from the pack."*

*"Sometimes I feel like rap music is almost the key to stopping racism."*

Marshall blew up after placing second in the 1997 Rap Olympics when a tape of his performance made its way to Dr. Dre.

**Big Sean (1988- ),** a.k.a. Sean Anderson, graduated from Cass Tech. After a chance meeting with Kanye West, Big Sean was challenged to rap 16 bars for him, which led to his signing to West's label two years later.

*"For me, personally, Detroit is a melting pot for everything. We get the best from the East Coast, West Coast and down South."*

*"Definitely just growing up in general influenced me; Detroit happened to be where I was. I feel like the city definitely has made an impact on my life and made me who I am. Detroit has an unmistakable soul – nobody can duplicate the soul we bring to the game. From Motown to J Dilla to Eminem to anything."*

*"My music is the essence of Detroit. At one time, we were the center of the world, man – Motor City."*

Sean received the key to the city for his work with city kids and Cass Tech.

**J Dilla (1974-2006),** or James Yancey, went to Pershing High School and was an influential producer and rapper, emerging from Detroit's underground scene in the 1990s as one of the founding members of acclaimed Slum Village.

*"I'm a record shopping fanatic. I already got a nice stash here and I got a warehouse full of records in Detroit, it's ridiculous."*

*"It's kinda fucked up because the audience we were trying to give to were actually people we hung around. Me, myself, I hung around regular ass Detroit cats."*

*"When I go in the studio, I just try to give the artist what they want."*

Despite his early death, Dilla still had several projects planned for the future and over 150 unreleased beats.

**Xzibit (1974- ),** was born Alvin Joiner in Detroit, before moving to Albuquerque, New Mexico, with his father after his mother's death.

*"I don't believe in aliens. I don't think aliens or ghosts like black people. We never get abducted; our houses never get haunted. It always happens in rural areas, where no ethnic people live. The day I see somebody from South Central Los Angeles say, 'Man, I got abducted yesterday,' then I'll believe it."*

Finding fame in the West Coast scene, Xzibit went on to host *Pimp My Ride*, which I watched regularly.

**Obie Trice (1977- ),** began his rap career at 14, attending the Hip Hop Shop, where he was discovered by Proof, a bandmate of Eminem. Trice signed with Eminem's Shady Records in 2000.

*"Detroit is right now a new Mecca for Hip Hop."*

*"I want to talk to those coming up in the 'hood, coming up in the struggle. We're killing each other, and it's about nothing. Nothing. Nothing. We're all dying... over nothing."*

*"7 Mile is like an Ave. Back in the days it was poppin' in the summer time."*

Upon Proof's death in 2005, Trice dedicated a song to him and spoke at his funeral against black-on-black violence.

**Danny Brown (1981- ),** or Daniel Sewell, always wanted to be a rapper. Influenced by his DJ father's interest in music, Danny was exposed to many forms of music early in life.

*"Since I was a kid, I'd wake up every morning hearing a voice say, 'You're the greatest rapper ever.' I'm trying to prove that voice right."*

*"From an early age, music was my only thing. You come from Detroit, you learn how to make the most of what you can do best."*

After struggling early in his career with different labels, Brown received attention with his four-volume mixtape *Detroit State of Mind*.

**Insane Clown Posse** was formed as a duo with **Violent J (1972- ),** a.k.a. Joseph Bruce, and **Shaggy 2 Dope (1974- ),** a.k.a., Joseph Utsler, in 1989. Appearing in clown makeup and throwing Faygo pop onto their audience, ICP developed a loyal following called "The Juggalos," who have been investigated by the FBI as a criminal gang.

*"We made the point that millions of people bought our albums, and out of millions of people, there is going to be some bad apples. I'm sure Barbra Streisand fans have committed crimes as well…"*

*"It was probably something along the lines of you can't throw Faygo or something. We might have been asked to perform on the tour, but we couldn't bring our Faygo because of whatever the reason was. That's always a deal breaker."*

After feuds with Eminem and Disney over their songs, ICP still marches on with their Juggalos firmly in tow.

## Techno

**The Electrifying Mojo (??- ??),** was a DJ in the late 1970s and 1980s on WGPR. Each show would kick off with the "Landing of The Mothership," a dramatic intro of Mojo returning to Detroit on a UFO every night. Although geared to a mostly black audience, the show was followed by anyone interested in new music.

*"When I first got to Detroit, it was like apartheid on the dial, separatist radio."*

*"When you feel like you're at the end of your rope, tie a knot and keep hanging on… and keep remembering, that there ain't nobody bad like you."*

Considered by Detroit's techno trio to be their biggest inspiration, the Electrifying Mojo is the original founder of Techno, in my opinion.

**Juan Atkins (1962- ),** is one of the originators of techno music, along with his partners, Derrick May and Kevin Saunderson. Heavily influenced by DJ pioneer, the Electrifying Mojo, the trio went on to acclaim throughout Europe for introducing a new style of music to the world.

*"When I first heard synthesizers dropped on records it was great… like UFOs landing on records, so I got one. It wasn't any one particular group that turned me on to synthesizers, but "Flashlight," by Parliament,*

*was the first record I heard where maybe 75 percent of the production was electronic."*

*"Maybe techno coming out of Detroit had more of the black experience involved, and of course what we've grown up with is soul music and R&B stuff, and then there's funk itself, it would be only natural that more of these elements would show up."*

Juan shares my view of the importance of the Electrifying Mojo or maybe I share his:

*"You'd sit there in a trance waiting for each record Mojo was going to play."*

*"He was an underground cult hero. We would listen to him religiously every night."*

**Derrick May (1963- ),** a.k.a. "Mayday," grew up in Detroit, moving to Belleville at 13. There he met Saunderson and Atkins, forming the DJ group, Deep Space Sounds.

*"We had a young beautiful black crowd and I mean beautiful in the sense of spirit mind and soul. We had white kids coming, Spanish kids coming, gay kids coming, straight kids coming."*

**Kevin Saunderson (1964- ),** met Derrick May in high school, in Belleville, outside Detroit. Their first encounter was a dispute over money in which Saunderson knocked May out cold.

*"I used to wake up in the middle of the night, go into my studio – which was in the next room – and lay down the ideas as they came to me. At the time, it was all about experimentation and being a college kid."*

**Carl Craig (1969- ),** went to Cooley High School and was influenced by Derrick May's radio show. Craig went on to record his own music as a producer for other artists.

*"I have a bad habit of getting my hands dirty in every little thing, and I really do enjoy it."*

When it comes to the Electrifying Mojo, Carl, Juan, and I think alike:

*"Mojo was a fantastic visionary."*

*"He had a spiritual intergalactic quality to him. Mojo was playing music from around the world that was so impactful, not commercially, but spiritually and creatively."*

Atkins, Saunderson and May are called the "Belleville Three," and are the originators of "Detroit Techno," while Craig came up in the second wave of artists. It was exciting to see a brand-new genre of music emerge from my city. The place produces geniuses, I tell you.

# ON SPORTS

*"I love sports. Whenever I can, I always watch the
Detroit Tigers on the radio."*
- Gerald R. Ford, 38th President

Sports are a big part of Detroit's identity and Detroiters
are loyal to a fault, following our teams through thick
and thin. We have seen the highs of success and
the lows of mediocrity, individual greatness, folly,
champions, triumphs, curses and stretches of failure.

## Detroit Tigers

**Ty Cobb, Outfielder, played 1905-1926,** Cobb
was the greatest to ever wear the Old English D. An
original member of the Hall of Fame, the "Georgia
Peach" left a legacy of hard, dominating play that
has yet to be matched.

*"When I came to Detroit I was just a mild-mannered
Sunday-school boy."*

*"When I began playing the game, baseball was about
as gentlemanly as a kick in the crotch."*

*"My system was all offense. I believed in putting up a mental hazard for the other fellow. If we were five or six runs ahead, I'd try some wild play, such as going from first to home on a single. This helped to make the other side hurry the play in a close game later on. I worked out all the angles I could think of, to keep them guessing and hurrying."*

To show you how ruthless Cobb could be, while in New York, he once climbed into the stands and attacked a fan who kept heckling him. The fan, a man named Claude Lucker, was handicapped (he had lost all of one hand and three fingers on his other hand in an industrial accident). When onlookers shouted at him to stop because the man had no hands, he reportedly retorted:

*"I don't care if he got no feet!"*

Cobb retired holding 90 MLB records, some of which still stand today. His ferocious play on the field matched his intolerance off the field.

**Schoolboy Rowe, Pitcher, played 1933-1942,** earned his nickname as a 15 year old boy playing on a men's team. A favorite in Detroit for his southern charm and superstitions, Rowe always picked up his glove with his left hand, kept charms in his pockets and was the first Tiger to talk to a ball. Admired for his public devotion to his high school sweet-heart, Rowe once asked his fiancé on a nationally broadcast interview:

*"How'm I doing, Edna honey?"*

*"Just eat a lot of vittles, climb on that mound, wrap my fingers around the ball and say to it, 'Edna, honey, let's go.'"*

Taunted by opposing players and fans for his simple but now famous line, his romance with Edna became a national fascination and they married after the 1934 season.

**Charlie Gerhinger, Second Base, played 1924-1942,** was one of the best second baseman to ever play the game. I knew the "Mechanical Man" for 30 years or more and never heard him utter more the 10 words at a time. Charlie kept a low profile among Detroit's other stars. Player-manager Mickey Cochrane joked that "Charlie says 'hello' on Opening Day, 'goodbye' on closing day, and in between hits .350." Remarking about fellow teammate Hank

Greenberg's talent for RBIs, Charlie once suggested to Hank:

*"You'd trip a runner coming around third base just so you could knock him in yourself."*

Asked why he signed his name "Chas. Gehringer," he responded,

*"Why use seven letters when four will do?"*

His full remarks, at an event honoring his career:

*"I'm known around baseball as saying very little, and I'm not going to spoil my reputation."*

Gerhinger enjoyed barnstorming with other Major Leaguers and one year joined a travelling group of Negro League players including Satchel Paige and Buck Leonard. Paige said that Gehringer was the best white hitter he ever pitched against.

**Hank Greenberg, First Base, played 1930, 1933-1941, 1945-1946,** was one of the greatest power hitters of his generation. "Hammerin' Hank" led the Tigers to four World Series, winning two. The first

Jewish baseball star, in 1934, he refused to play on Rosh Hashanah but relented after consulting his rabbi. Fans groused, "Rosh Hashanah comes every year but the Tigers haven't won the pennant since 1909." In 1940, Hank became the first American League player to register for the draft. Greenberg served 47 months, more than any other player.

*"I made up my mind to go when I was called. My country comes first."*

He returned from the war in time to lead the Tigers to a World Series win in 1945.

**George Kell, Third Base, played 1946-1952, broadcaster, 1959-1963, 1965-1996,** played for the Tigers for six years, winning the 1949 batting title with a .343 average. His southern folksy style as an announcer was beloved by many fans. His favorite story was about the time Joe DiMaggio broke his jaw on a line drive hit.

*"I got up, made the play at third, then passed out."*

Kell is best known around here as the TV voice of the Tigers for more than 30 years.

**Al Kaline, Outfielder, played 1953-1974,** had more than 3,000 hits and 18 Gold Gloves in his career playing right field. At eight years old he developed osteomyelitis and had a segment of bone removed from his left foot. The surgery left him with scarring and permanent deformity. He played his first ten years on a crippled left foot. In 1964, he finished second for the American League Most Valuable Player award, after the season, upon finally having surgery, he exclaimed,

*"I feel so much better than I did before, that it's ridiculous."*

"Mr. Tiger" was the best right fielder to ever play the game. His demeanor was even greater – the most pleasant man that you'll ever meet.

**Willie Horton, Outfielder, played 1963-1977,** hit his first home run in Tiger Stadium at the age of 16, leading Detroit Northwestern High School to the city championship. Idolized by many in Detroit's African-American community for playing for the hometown team, Willie walked through the crowds wearing his uniform during the 1967 riots pleading for peace and an end to the violence.

*"Maybe, that was the night I embraced my community for the first time as an adult."*

*"To this day, the only thing I remember is people telling us to go straight home. And then the next thing I know, I still have my uniform on and I was out in the middle of the riots."*

*"People recognized me that night, and later some would thank me for at least making an effort."*

Horton, my favorite Tiger, had a powerful swing, sometime hitting one-handed home runs. He is venerated as one of the Detroit Tiger greats.

**Mickey Lolich, Pitcher, played 1963-1975,** was named MVP of the 1968 World Series, in which he pitched three complete games. I used to join him and the boys down at the Lindell AC after games.

*"All the fat guys watch me and say to their wives, See, there's a fat guy doing okay."*

*"Bring me another beer."*

A tricycle accident as a child forced him to throw left handed, but he wrote and batted right handed.

**Denny McClain, Pitcher, played 1963-1970,** was asked about his teammate Mickey Lolich's three complete game wins in the 1968 World Series, the last on two days rest, beating the great Bob Gibson of the St. Louis Cardinals.

*"I wouldn't trade one Bob Gibson for twelve Mickey Loliches."*

Denny won the Cy Young and American League Most Valuable Player awards in 1968, posting a 31-6 record. He was the first player to do so since Dizzy Dean in 1934, becoming the last player and one of only eleven to ever to do so.

**Ernie Harwell, Broadcaster, 1960-2002,** was the voice of the Tigers for a couple generations.

*"The greatest single moment I've ever known in Detroit was Jim Northrup's triple in the seventh game of the World Series in St. Louis. It was a stunning moment because not only were the Tigers winning a world championship that meant so much to an entire city, they were beating the best pitcher I ever saw – Bob Gibson."*

An icon in sports broadcasting, Ernie was a dedicated

champion of baseball history. His collection is in the Detroit Main Library and covers more than 60 years of first-hand baseball history.

**Norm Cash, First Base, played 1960-1974,** was a powerful left-handed bat and great fielder, leading the 1968 Tigers to a World Series win.

*"Pro-rated at 500 at-bats per year, my 1,081 strike-outs would mean that for 2 years out of the 14 I played, I never touched the ball."*

*"I owe my success to expansion pitching, a short right field fence, and my hollow bats."*

The first player to hit a ball out of Tiger Stadium, "Stormin' Norman" hit the ball out onto Trumbull four times in his career.

**William "Gates" Brown, Outfielder, played 1963-1975,** a huge contributor to the 1968 World Series Champion team, Gates still holds the batting average record as a pinch hitter in a season at .450.

*"In high school, I took a little English, some science, some hubcaps and some wheel covers."*

In one game, realizing he was not starting, he bought two hot dogs and then was called on to bat. After stuffing the hot dogs into his uniform, he drove a ball into the outfield. Upon sliding into second base, he got up covered in ketchup, mustard and smashed hot dogs and buns.

**Billy Martin, Manager, managed 1971-1973,** was known for his pugnacious attitude and had a reputation for post-game drinking brawls. He is credited with discovering Ron LeFlore, who was incarcerated in Jackson State Prison at the time. Earning a pardon by signing with the Tigers, Ron became a great base stealer and played centerfield. When another player voiced his concerns about LeFlore's past, Billy responded:

*"Where do you think they found Gates Brown? In kindergarten?"*

Billy managed the Tigers to the 1972 American League Championship, falling to World Series Champs, the Oakland Athletics, three games to two. As he was being photographed for his 1972 baseball card, Martin gave the photographer the finger, going undiscovered until after its release.

**Mark "The Bird" Fidrych, Pitcher, played 1976-1980,** was one of the few bright spots during a bad stretch in the 1970s.

*"When you're a winner, you're always happy, but if you're happy as a loser, you'll always walk away a loser."*

Nicknamed "The Bird" for his spastic, animated pitching, he endeared fans by talking to the ball before pitches. A one-year wonder, his career was cut short by a rotator cuff injury that went undiagnosed.

**Jack Morris, Pitcher, played 1977-1990,** led the Tigers, to the 1984 World Series Championship, On April 7th of that year he pitched Detroit's first no-hitter since 1958. Flamboyant and outspoken, he never shied away from confrontation. Once approached by a woman reporter in the clubhouse after a game, he told her:

*"I don't talk to women when I'm naked unless they're on top of me or I'm on top of them."*

After mastering the split-finger fastball, he became a dominant pitcher throughout the 1980s.

**Kirk Gibson, Outfielder, played 1983-1987,** was part of one of the greatest moments in World Series history. Facing San Diego Padres pitcher Goose Gosasge in the World Series-clinching game, Gibson hit a three-run homer in the 8th inning, winning the series for the Tigers.

*"I flashed ten fingers and yelled back to Sparky, 'ten bucks they pitch to me and I crank it.'"*

Having struck out Gibson in his first at bat in the Major Leagues, Gossage told his catcher that he "owned" Gibson. I don't think Tiger Stadium was ever as loud when he hit that home run.

**Sparky Anderson, Manager, managed 1979-1995,** was Detroit baseball's greatest ambassador. Throughout 1984, the Tigers led the American League. That year remains one of my favorite Tiger memories. In a pivotal game in the World Series, he remarked to Kirk Gibson as he walked up to face Goose Gossage:

*"He don't want to walk you!"*

His 1984 Tigers started the year, 35-5, a record, and won the World Series.

*"I knew then it was all over, and to be honest I realized I would be the first manager to win a World Series in both leagues."*

Remarking on his last few years as manager before retiring, Sparky said:

*"It's a terrible thing to have to tell your fans, who have waited like Detroit's have, that their team won't win it this year. But it's better than lying to them."*

*"The great thing about baseball is when you are done, you'll only tell your grandchildren the good things. If they ask me about 1989 I'll tell them I had amnesia."*

Despite ownership's dismantling of the World Series team, losing many great players during the 1980s, Sparky remained loyal to the game and the fans of Detroit. A class act, he never showed his disappointment.

**Jim Leyland, Manager, managed 2006-2013,** started his career as a catcher in 1963 with the Tigers. Leyland became manager of their AAA farm team in 1979 to 1981, grooming the players that won the 1984 World Series.

*"My eight years in Detroit, obviously, were my most successful years managing. We kinda rekindled the fire of baseball in Pittsburgh. We did the exact same thing in Detroit."*

Jimmy won over 700 games with the Tigers, and took Detroit to three consecutive American League Central Division Titles, and two World Series, falling short as champions both times.

## Detroit Lions

**Earl "Dutch" Clark, Quarterback, played 1934-38,** led the Lions to their first title in 1935. Red Grange said, "he was the hardest man in football to tackle." His last two seasons, he was a player-coach. After a grueling loss in 1937, he announced his retirement.

*"I'm too old. Look how long it takes me to get undressed."*

"The Flying Dutchman" was one of the greatest players in the early years of the NFL.

**Gerald R. Ford, Center, University of Michigan, played 1932-1935,** led two national-title teams for the Wolverines, in 1932 and 1933, but Ford, a College

All-Star, rejected offers by the pros, preferring to pursue a graduate degree instead.

*"I had pro offers from the Detroit Lions and Green Bay Packers, who were pretty hard up for linemen in those days. If I had gone into professional football the name Jerry Ford might have been a household word today."*

Ford served in the House of Representatives from 1949 to 1973, representing the Grand Rapids area. Upon Richard Nixon's resignation, Ford became the 38th President of the United States. Mocked for his clumsiness as president, Ford was one of the most athletic presidents in history.

**Bobby Layne, Quarterback, played 1950-1958,** led the Lions to three championships – in 1952, in 1953, and their last in 1957 – falling short of a three-peat in 1954, with a loss to Cleveland by a score of 56-10. Layne remarked after the game-

*"I slept too much last night."*

Known for his heavy drinking, he didn't really show up until he sobered up in the second half.

*"If I'd known I was gonna live this long, I'd have taken a lot better care of myself."*

Traded mid-season in 1958, Layne was furious. As Detroit's famed leader on and off the field, Bobby loved Detroit and remained bitter about being traded.

*"I'd like to win a championship for the Steelers and for myself to shove down Detroit's throat."*

It's been rumored that upon learning of the trade, Layne put a curse on the team, and for the next 50 years, the Lions had the worst winning percentage in football.

*"The Lions won't win for another 50 years."*

Well, I'm here to confirm it as true.

**Doak Walker, Running Back, played 1950-55,** became Rookie of the Year in 1950, and later was voted to the NFL Hall of Fame. Earlier, he'd been a teammate of Bobby Layne's at Highland Park High in Dallas. Commenting on his longtime friend's habit for winning games after a disastrous first half performance, Walker once remarked:

*"Bobby never lost a game in his life, time just ran out on him."*

I was sorry to see Doak retire so early. He was one of the most gifted running backs in the game.

**Dick "Night Train" Lane, Defensive Back, played 1960-1965,** was prodigious at intercepting passes. He still ranks fourth all time with 68 career interceptions. The "Night Train Necktie," also known as a clothesline tackle, was later banned because of its violent impact.

*"My object is to stop the guy before he gains another inch... If I hit them in the legs they may fall forward for a first down... I grab them around the neck so I can go back to the bench and sit down."*

*"I hope the black players will band together to deal with the problem of no black coaches, no black managers and few black quarterbacks in pro football."*

Upon his retirement, Lane became the first African-American in the Lions front office.

**Alex Karras, Defensive Tackle, played 1958-1970,** was one of the great lineman of his era. Alex played with an edge. Missing only one game in his 12-year career, Alex led a dominating defense. Surrounded by controversy, Alex was suspended for the 1963 season for betting on games with Paul Hornung, the Packer great. Returning the next year, he refused to call the pregame coin toss, telling the ref:

*"I'm sorry, sir. I'm not permitted to gamble."*

He made his film debut in George Plimpton's *Paper Lion* in 1968. After retiring, he went on to a successful Hollywood career, best known for punching a horse in *Blazing Saddles*.

**Monte Clark, Coach, coached 1978-1984,** was considered one of the top emerging coaches when he arrived in 1978, but like most Lions coaches, his tenure seemed cursed. Although he did win a division title and took the team to the playoffs, the Lions lost the lead in the final minutes and then the game as Lions kicker Eddie Murray missed a 43-yard field goal in the final seconds. On the sidelines before the kick, it appeared that Clark was praying. Regarding his unanswered prayer, Clark said:

*"It was answered, but the answer was No."*

*"The key to this whole business is sincerity. Once you can fake that, you've got it made."*

Monte never coached again and was out of football for five years after his stint with the Lions.

**Jeff Komlo, Quarterback, played 1979-1981,** was the first rookie who was not drafted number-one by his team to ever start the first game in a season. Yet Komlo had a terrible career and an even more unfortunate life. In August 2005, while on the lam for two DUI convictions, Komlo was also wanted for drug possession, assault and suspected of arson. While on the run, he worked at a hair implant clinic.

*"I'm not a criminal."*

He was killed in an automobile crash in 1989. Authorities first suspected he faked his own death to avoid the charges.

**Darryl Rogers, Coach, coached 1985-1988,** was another in a long line of coaching failures.

*"What's it take to get fired around here anyhow?"*

The fact that Rogers hung around so long is a testament to Lions owner William Clay Ford's loyalty and stupidity.

**Wayne Fontes, Coach, coached 1989-1996,** led the team with most wins in history, 67. Fontes also led the franchise with the most losses, 71. Another hapless leader with a tenure that stretched way too long, Fontes was notable for his humor and for fans' ridicule.

*"I'm like that big buck that's in the field. They're trying to hunt him down, trying to shoot him. I just keep dodging those bullets. Everybody wants my rack on the wall."*

*"Our offense today set football back 100 years."*

*"Well, first it was 7-7 and then I turned around and it was 31-7."*

*"Our defense did not play very well. What we did not want to happen, happened."*

This about sums up the legacy of the Fontes era.

**Jerry Ball, Nose Tackle, played 1987-1992,** was a three-time Pro Bowler and a powerhouse at nose tackle. Throughout his career, he was always double or triple-teamed.

*"It seemed like our defense was out on the field a game and a half."*

Jerry earned his Pro Bowl status on the famed Wayne Fontes-led teams.

**Lomas Brown, Offensive Tackle, played 1985-1995,** started all but one of his 164 starts for the Lions. Known for his durability, Brown led the offensive line, opening holes for the great Barry Sanders.

*"It was three plays and out, three and out, three and out over and over, punt, punt, punt."*

A fixture on the offensive line for a decade, Lomas returned to Detroit as a broadcaster, offering color commentary on Lion games.

**Chris Spielman, Linebacker, played 1988-1995,** finished his career as the leader in tackles for the Lions with 1,138. During his career, the Lions won two division titles and played in the 1991 NFC Championship game.

*"It's not fun for anybody."*

One of the best in Lion's history, Spielman followed in the footsteps of the great Lion middle linebacker

Joe Schmidt, one of the best-ever, and credited with developing the position.

**Deion Sanders, Receiver, Florida State University,** when told he was considered by the Lions as possible draft pick in 1989, said he hated the idea of going to perennial loser Detroit.

*"I was kinda scared. I thought Detroit was gonna take me. I would've asked them for so much money they would have to put me on layaway."*

Fortunately for the Lions, their 1989 draft pick was Barry Sanders.

**Barry Sanders, Running Back, played 1989-1998,** was the greatest Lion ever. Sanders, never one for individual achievements, retired before he broke Walter Payton's record for most yards all-time. Suffering through losing season after losing season, Barry always had an answer.

*"I don't have the answer."*

*"I quit because I didn't feel like the Detroit Lions had a chance to win. It just killed my enjoyment of the game."*

*"I hope this is the low point."*

Fed up with the direction the Lions were heading after reaching the 1991 NFC Championship game, Sanders retired by fax to his hometown newspaper in Wichita.

**Brett Perriman, Receiver, played 1991-1996,** and Herman Moore were the first wide receiver duo to post 1,400 yards each in a season.

*"We stunk the place up."*

Despite the talent and firepower of Detroit's offense, the team went nowhere, as usual.

**Erik Kramer, Quarterback, played 1991-1993,** got his start in pro football by playing as a scab during the 1987 players strike.

*"I joined the Lions initially wanting to solidify that No. 3 spot behind Rodney and Andre."*

I guess you can't fault anyone if they have little talent and want to play football. After all, third string would be a pretty good paycheck. But if that is your dream in this world, to play behind Andre Ware, then your goals are pretty small.

**Johnnie Morton, Receiver, played 1994-2001,** was another great receiver in a high-powered offense that set records but not wins.

*"It seemed like every play, someone wasn't there."*

Johnnie ranks third in Lions history in receptions and yards receiving. Another talent lost to the Detroit curse.

**Scott Mitchell, Quarterback, played 1994-1998,** had a successful season replacing Dan Marino of the Dolphins before he arrived in Detroit as the quarterback of the future, but he struggled his first year. So frustrated with his play, Tackle Lomas Brown purposefully missed a block, ending Mitchell's season.

*"Why? I have no explanations."*

In 1995, he set single season records for touchdown passes and passing yards, fueling a high-energy offense with Barry Sanders and Herman Moore.

**Bobby Ross, Coach, coached 1997-2000,** joined the Lions as the team searched for more structure and leadership from their coach. But after years of the Fontes effect, the players revolted at the restrictions he imposed, resenting the tougher practices, weightlifting regimens and curfews.

*"We want our checks and that's good enough for us. Winning isn't that important as long as we get our paycheck."*

*"You think I coach that?"*

*"You'd think I just rolled out of bed today and have no history with coaching and with players."*

*"We took a licking at the line of scrimmage, and just about everywhere else, too."*

Resigning mid-season, Ross gave up on the team. Unable to change the mentality of the players, he became adversarial, accusing them of being soft and lacking effort.

**Charlie Batch, Quarterback, played 1998-2001,** came to Detroit and witnessed the retirement of Barry Sanders in his prime, the unraveling of the front office and the beginning of the Matt Millen era.

*"I have no answers."*

Batch is rated sixth overall in Lions history, passing for over 9,000 yards, yet was deemed ineffective by Millen as he completely remade the roster.

**Matt Millen, General Manager, managed 2001-2008,** proves that a great player and bombastic announcer does not make a successful GM. The Millen years, during which he was the second-highest paid executive in the league, were some of the hardest for fans who have been through so many disappointments. Some of his wisdom:

*"He did a couple things today in practice and I sat there, and I just wanted to grab him by the throat and choke him."*

*"Then you get into the game and it's like, where are your testicles?"*

*"You faggot, yeah you heard me, you faggot."*

*"What I said was stupid and wrong, I would hope I learned a big lesson because those words were careless."*

*"I don't want to say anything, I'll wind up regretting it."*

*"Well, I have a guy right now who I believe is a devout coward."*

The Fords stood by him for years, despite his constant failures at drafting and signing talent.

**Roy Williams, Receiver, played 2004-2008,** was notable for being the second of three receivers drafted by Millen in the first round in three consecutive seasons, sandwiched by such failures as Charles Rogers and Mike Williams. Roy at least had enough productive years that he became trade bait.

*"Is this team cursed?"*

One of three over-reaches by Matt Millen in search of a star receiver, Williams at least made the Pro Bowl in 2007.

**Rod Marinelli, Coach, coached 2006-2008,** was the fourth coach hired by Matt Millen, who failed the previous times in finding a leader. His final season, the Lions went 0-16, the first winless season since the 16-game schedule was initiated.

*"You can't go 0-16 and expect to keep your job."*

At 10-38 over three seasons, Marinelli has one of the worst records over three years in the history of the NFL.

**William Clay Ford, Owner, owned 1963-2014,** could not translate brilliance in the boardroom to achievement in sports. After taking over the Lions six years from their last championship in 1957, the Lions under Ford's ownership went 54 years with only one playoff win and only 11 playoff appearances.

*"A ragtag operation."*

*"We take two hours sending in the wrong plays."*

*"We're boring and we're losing. I can't think of two worse adjectives to apply to the way we're playing."*

*"Detroit – and I'm not blowing smoke at anybody – is probably the greatest fan sports town in the country. They'll support anything."*

*"What do you want me to do, fire myself? I'm not going to."*

As much as I'd like to, I won't bash Mr. Ford. He was a gracious man, smart in business and a great benefactor for this city. He truly loved owning the team and wanted more than anything success, on the field.

## Detroit Red Wings

**Jack Adams, Coach and GM, coached 1927-1947, managed 1927-1963,** began his career coaching in Detroit when the team was named the Cougars. In 1931 they became the Falcons. Finally, in 1932, the team began playing as the Detroit Red Wings. Nicknamed "Trader Jack," Adams was known for blockbuster trades, believing it kept the players on edge to perform.

*"If it's free, it's advice; if you pay for it, it's counseling; if you can use either one, it's a miracle."*

He is the only man to have his name on the Stanley Cup as a player, coach and general manager.

**Gordie Howe, Right Wing, played 1946-1971,** was known as "Mr. Hockey." Despite playing in an era known for defense, Howe is in the Top Ten in most career scoring categories. Considered the greatest all-around player in history, Howe's career spanned six decades.

*"All pro athletes are bilingual. They know English and profanity."*

*"If you find you can push someone around, then you push him around."*

The "Gordie Howe Hat Trick" consisting of a goal, assist and a fight, became part of his legend, although he only ever recorded two of them.

**Ted Lindsay, Right Wing, played 1944-1960, 1964-1965,** earned the nickname "Terrible Ted" for his toughness on the ice.

*"By 1946, I knew Detroit was the best hockey city in the Original six."*

*"I had the idea that I should beat up every player I tangled with and nothing ever convinced me it wasn't a good idea."*

Credited with organizing the NHL Players Association with Montreal Canadien defenseman Doug Harvey, Ted fought for the players to have negotiating rights and pensions, improving their conditions.

*"Actually, we don't have many grievances. We just felt we should have an organization of this kind."*

*"They thought we were going to hurt the game, but we just wanted to help ourselves, because the players needed to get together to protect their interests."*

*"What you had at the time was a dictatorship with the team owners."*

Elected to the Hall of Fame in 1966, he refused to attend the men-only event without his wife and family. The next year the rules were changed.

**Red Kelly, Defenseman, played 1947-1960,** won four Stanley Cups with the Red Wings and eight regular season championships. He played the 1959 season with a broken ankle. A reporter asked why he didn't play as well as previous years.

*"Don't know. Might have been the ankle."*

GM Jack Adams traded him for revealing the secret broken ankle.

**Terry Sawchuck, Goalie, played 1949-1964, 1968-1969,** compiled a record of 447 wins. A record which lasted for thirty years. Terry played in the era without masks or backups.

*"The day they put me in net I had a good game. I've stayed there ever since."*

*"We are the sort of people that make health insurance popular."*

In 1962, Sawchuck finally donned a facemask during games. Four years later, *Life* magazine had a makeup artist apply stitches and scars to his face demonstrating his more than 400 stitches, including three to his right eyeball, and his multiple scars that he received playing without a mask.

**Alex Delvecchio, Center / Right Wing, played 1950-1973, Coach, coached 1973-1977,** spent his entire career in Detroit and, upon his retirement, was second all-time in games played, assists and points in NHL history. Delvecchio became the Red Wings coach after he retired.

*"It would have been worse if we hadn't blocked the kick after Toronto's second touchdown."*

Alex is one of only three NHL players to play more than 1,500 games with one team, Red Wing greats Yzerman and Lidstrom are the other two.

**Mickey Redmond, Right Wing, played 1970-1976, broadcaster, 1979-present,** was the first Red Wing to score more than 50 goals in a season. He was beloved by fans for his "Mickeyisms."

*"He got the whole jar of mustard on that one!"*

*"He can't get out of his own way!"*

*"He was standing there like a cigar store Indian!"*

*"Get that lunch bucket shined up and go to work!"*

With a potential Hall of Fame career cut short by injury, Mick joined the Hall of Fame as a broadcaster.

**Steve Yzerman, Center, played 1983-2006,** was known as "The Captain." Stevie Y retired as the longest serving captain of any team in North American Major League Sports history. Drafted fourth overall by new team owners Mike and Marian Illitch in their first draft, Yzerman brought the team back from mediocrity, beginning a 25-year run in the playoffs. He led Detroit to three Stanley Cups, winning a fourth as a VP in the front office, and is considered one of the greatest Red Wings players ever.

*"I consider the Detroit Red Wings one of the greatest franchises in any sport. For a player to come in and play, it's so special to wear the jersey."*

*"It's been a great honor for me to be a player for the Detroit Red Wings, to play for an Original Six franchise. I know I'm far from perfect, but I learned a lot."*

*"Very few cities in the NHL have the history or the following of the Detroit Red Wings."*

Stevie led by example. Quiet in the dressing room, he let his play inspire his teammates. Yzerman returned Detroit to its rightful place as one of hockey's elite teams. The team was so successful, Detroit became known as "Hockeytown."

**Bob Probert, Left Wing, played 1985-1994,** and Joe Kocur were known as the "Bruise Brothers." Bob was one of the fiercest enforcers, hockey's name for a player with more skills fighting than playing. A hard hitter and even harder partier, Bob got into more than his share of trouble outside the law.

*"Trust me, I'm a really nice guy."*

*"Just charge me with the usual."*

His off the ice activities led to his dismissal from Detroit.

**Stu Grimson, Left Wing, played 1994-1997,** was another enforcer. "The Grim Reaper" would be called out to protect the more skilled players from opponents' pounding checks. Explaining why he kept a color photo of himself above his locker, he said:

*"That's so when I forget how to spell my name, I can still find my clothes."*

With so many skill and finesse players on the Red Wings, Grimson offered a trait that was necessary during this era of hockey. The fighting and hitting was so punishing, Stu suffered multiple concussions, even blacking out during a game.

**Nick Lidstrom, Defenseman, played 1987-2012,** is the greatest defenseman to ever play the game.

*"You have to pay attention to details to have success in the playoffs. You can't take anyone lightly."*

*"Retiring today allows me to walk away from the game with pride, rather than have the game walk away from me."*

The first European Captain to win a Stanley Cup, Nick also holds the record for most games played for a single team.

## Detroit Pistons

**Dave DeBusschere, Forward and Coach, played 1962-1968, coached 1964-1967,** was a star at the University of Detroit. One of only 12 athletes to play in both the NBA and Major League Baseball, Dave joined the Pistons as a rookie in 1962. He became a player-coach at age 24 in the 1964-65 season, the youngest coach ever in the NBA.

*"The best teams have chemistry. They communicate with each other and they sacrifice personal glory for a common goal."*

After playing, Dave became commissioner of the rival ABA in the 1975-76 season. He is credited with merging the two rival leagues.

**Spencer Haywood, Power Forward, played 1968-1969, University of Detroit,** turned pro after his sophomore season, his only year as a Titan. His 21.5 rebounds per game and his 32.1 scoring average were tops in the NCAA. At the time, NBA rules forbid underclassman from joining the league. He then joined the ABA and, in 1970, sued the NBA to join the Seattle Supersonics. Spencer's anti-trust lawsuit against the NBA went all the way to the Supreme Court before a settlement was reached.

*"The real superstar is a man or a woman raising six kids on $150 a week."*

*"I'm not in the Hall of Fame, and I'm not going to be in the Hall of Fame... The word from the NBA is that I'm too controversial. Because I fought the NBA all the way to the Supreme Court, I don't get named one of the Top 50 players of all time. I'm supposed to be erased out of all history – and I have been erased."*

Despite his great talent, the NBA never forgot, nor forgave him.

**Dave Bing, Point Guard, played 1966-1975,** led the Pistons to four straight postseasons but could not get past the second round. Suffering an eye injury as a young boy, Bing played with a fuzzy left eye throughout his career.

*"I'm a better free-throw shooter because I've had to practice more on it."*

*"I figure I'd better be doing something in case I can't score enough."*

*"Basketball is a psyche game. You psyche the other guy. Some men talk. Other guys push. It's not to get you riled, not to hurt you. It isn't a test of manhood, not to me. Just a test of skills. Some nights, when things go well, then it's beautiful. It's togetherness. It's love."*

One of the greatest Pistons, Bing embraced the city, returning to Detroit after his playing days. He became a successful businessman and later became mayor.

**Bob Lanier, Center, played 1970-1980,** was drafted number-one overall and became an eight-time All-Star. His shoe, size 22, is featured at the Naismith Hall of Fame so visitors can compare their foot size to his.

*"Greatest moment? To me – and I know that this might sound a little trite – the greatest moment is that basketball has enabled me to touch other people's lives. I've always been able to do that. Since day one, being an NBA player and visiting a hospital or going to a senior citizens' home and listening to an elderly person who has much more wisdom than I'll ever have and brightening their day and giving*

*my energy. It's something that is very, very special that the NBA has been able to do. It's terrific for me."*

One of my favorite Pistons, Bob played some classic games against Kareem Abdul-Jabbar when he played for the Milwaukee Bucks. Legend has it that Lanier would smoke cigarettes during halftime. Knowing this, Kareem used to force Lanier to run more in the second half, seeking an advantage.

**George Gervin, Small Forward, played 1974-1986,** is one of the greatest shooting guards in NBA history. The "Iceman," so named for his cool demeanor on the court, is credited with developing the "finger roll," a technique where one rolls the ball off the tips of his fingers.

*"If one person did it, it's possible that someone else can accomplish the same feat."*

Gervin was a high school stand-out, averaging 31 points and 20 rebounds his senior year at Martin Luther King High School, and is largely considered one of the best to ever come out of Detroit.

**Marvin Barnes, Power Forward, played 1976-1977,** was nicknamed "Bad News" for his off-court problems. Playing only one season in Detroit, Barnes was arrested at Metro Airport with a gun in his bag, violating his probation. He served 152 days.

*"I'm a basketball player, not a monk."*

*"I ain't getting on no time machine."*

Upon his release, he was arrested again, this time for burglary, drug possession and trespassing, thus ending his short stint as a Piston.

**Dick Vitale, Coach, coached 1978-1979, University of Detroit, coached 1973-1977,** earned local hero status during his four years at the University of Detroit, 1973-1977. In his first year as Piston coach, Vitale drafted his two star Titan players, John Long and Terry Tyler, to the team. After a mediocre year, Vitale traded away two first round picks and star player, M.L. Carr, for an injured and worn out Bob McAdoo. This was his undoing.

*"Twelve for 23... It doesn't take a genius to see that's under 50 percent."*

*"A winner is someone who can look in the mirror at the end of the day and say in pursuit of my goal and dreams I gave my best."*

*"Life is simple. Make good decisions and good things happen. Make bad decisions and bad things happen."*

*"A loser is someone who makes excuses and alibis and blames everyone else for their losses and failures."*

*"The glory of sport is witnessing a well-coached team perform as a single unit, striving for a common goal and ultimately bringing distinction to the jersey the players represent."*

Although Vitale never coached again, his basketball knowledge and intense personality served him well as a TV announcer for college basketball games.

**Isaiah Thomas, Point Guard, played 1981-1994,** was the second pick in the 1981 NBA draft and instantly became the face and leader of the Pistons. His toughness became a Piston trademark. Thomas led the "Bad Boys" to two NBA Championships.

*"It was important to me to believe, because if I don't believe, how can I expect them to believe?"*

*"My greatest gift that I have in life is basketball."*

*"If all I'm remembered for is being a good basketball player, then I've done a bad job with the rest of my life."*

*"To answer that question honestly, I'd have to lie to you."*

*"Basketball is not played simply with X's and O's. It's played with both trust and confidence."*

Thomas brought excitement and a winning attitude to a team that never experienced success until his arrival. With a boyish face, and charm, Thomas became a fan favorite. His famous smile belied his intensity on the court.

**Chuck Daly, Coach, coached 1983-1992,** took the Pistons to the playoffs every year he coached, reaching the Finals three times and winning two NBA Championships.

*"Coaching is like flying an airplane, there is going to be a lot of turbulence, but your job is to land the plane safely."*

*"The first shot does not beat you."*

*"Though I'd have to say it was generally the guys in Detroit, as a group, that won the two Championships. They were terrific and I always look back very fondly."*

*"The less determined and the less motivated weed themselves out."*

Daly led the Pistons to respectability for the first time in their history. The team was feared for their punishing play. A dapper dresser, he was always the most well-dressed person in the arena.

**Joe Dumars, Shooting Guard and GM, played 1985-1999, managed 2000-2014,** was a six-time All-Star and four-time All-Defensive first team. Joe was known for his tenacious defense. Michael Jordan said Joe was the best defender he ever faced.

*"It's always cool to be a part of anything that hasn't happened before. This is a great sports town, and the fans around here are about to really have some fun following both teams."*

*"On good teams, coaches hold players accountable, on great teams players hold players accountable."*

*"We can talk about the value of sportsmanship on one hand, and on the other hand, the leading shots, highlights ... you see every night are the outrageous and unsportsmanlike, so I think there is a double*

standard here. On the one hand, we complain about it, on the other hand it's the first thing you see every night."

With a quiet demeanor, Dumars was the first recipient of the NBA Sportsmanship Award, now named the Joe Dumars Award. Joe D was the first African-American GM to win an NBA Championship.

**Grant Hill, Small Forward, played 1994-2000,** was considered one of best all-around players through college. Rookie of the Year, Grant twice led the voting for the All-Star Game. Through his first six seasons, only Oscar Robertson and LeBron James have posted better numbers.

*"Parents, they're strict on you when you're little, and you don't understand why. But as you get older, you understand and you appreciate it."*

*"The great thing about sports is you constantly have to prove yourself. You constantly have to go out there and do it, day in and day out."*

*"Yelling doesn't get your point across, it only makes it louder."*

In his last season with Detroit, Hill injured his left ankle right before the playoffs. Despite multiple surgeries, Hill could never return to his previous levels. He was traded to Orlando in a blockbuster trade that brought Ben Wallace to the Pistons.

**Doug Collins, Coach, coached 1995-1998,** was hired to groom Grant Hill, Detroit's new superstar. As coach for the Chicago Bulls, Doug mentored a young Michael Jordan through his first few years.

*"Any time Detroit scores more than 100 points and hold the other team below 100 points they almost always win."*

During his career in Chicago, Collins's Bulls, with Jordan, could never beat Detroit's "Bad Boys," frustrating Jordan, which led to Doug's dismissal in Chicago.

**Ben Wallace, Center, played 2000-2006,** became a powerhouse defensive player and rebounder leading the Pistons to their third Championship in 2004. Named Defensive Player of the Year four times, Ben was a rebounding machine.

*"Right now, I'm not really thinking about any of that. I'm just out here trying to have fun, play basketball."*

*"All that hard work is nothing if we don't continue to play the way we've played."*

*"Everybody's focus here is to win a championship. If we don't take that energy into the playoffs, it'd be a wasted season."*

Whenever "Big Ben" scored or blocked a shot, the Palace would play a deep chime, an imitation of London's Big Ben Tower.

**Rasheed Wallace, Power Forward, played 2004-2009,** was traded to Detroit one game into the 2003-04 season. He was the last piece of the puzzle for Detroit, as they won the NBA Championship that year.

*"Our ultimate goal, is not to have the best record, but to win that championship."*

*"It's no statement. It's just another game. Statements won't be made until the playoffs."*

*"It's not frustrating if you win."*

*"I'm not a big fan of individuality. My wife and kids will like it, but I'd rather have a championship."*

Wallace is the all-time leader in technical fouls. Although Detroit went to six consecutive Conference finals, they could not repeat their Championship success in 2004.

**Alan Iverson, Point Guard, played 2008-2009,** only played one year for Detroit and soon lost playing time to younger players. Not happy coming off the bench, Iverson was deactivated and then traded.

*"Detroit was a bad situation for me."*

A great player early in his career, Iverson was toxic to the chemistry of the team.

## Boxing

**Joe Louis, boxed, 1934-1951,** was the greatest heavyweight fighter of all time, reigning as the heavyweight champion for 1937-1949, the longest span of any heavyweight. Experiencing the racist backlash of Jack Johnson's reign as the first black champion, he was denied a title fight at first by the white powerbrokers of the time but soon became a symbol of pride for African-Americans during the depression. With his defeat of Max Schmeling, in

1938, Louis became a national hero and destroyed the Nazi theory of Aryan supremacy.

*"Lots of things wrong with America, but Hitler ain't going to fix them."*

*"Yeah, I'm scared. I'm scared I might kill Schmeling."*

*"He can run, but he can't hide."*

*"You have to be tough and stick it out, or you wind up being nothing."*

*"Every man got a right to his own mistakes. Ain't no man that ain't made any."*

*"You need a lot of different types of people to make the world better."*

*"Everybody wants to go to heaven, but nobody wants to die."*

*"If you gotta tell them who you are, you ain't nobody."*

Despite his elevation to national hero after defeating Schmeling, and his efforts to cultivate a non-threatening image, Louis suffered multiple acts of racism and segregation throughout his life, yet continued breaking barriers, finishing his boxing career at 66-3-1.

**Sugar Ray Robinson, boxed, 1940-1965,** is considered "pound for pound" the greatest fighter of all time. Sugar Ray spent his youth in Detroit, living on the same street as his idol, Joe Louis, for a time.

*"You always say 'I'll quit when I start to slide,' and then one morning you wake up and realize you've done slid."*

*"To be a champ you have to believe in yourself when no one else will."*

*"Don't let anything without a heart beat you."*

His six-fight battle with Jake LaMotta was legendary, splitting victories in two fights held in Detroit's Olympia Stadium three weeks apart in February 1943.

**Tommy Hearns, boxed, 1977-2006,** was known as the "Hitman" and the "Motor City Cobra." Coming out of Emanuel Steward's renowned Kronk Gym, Tommy was the first boxer in history to become World Champion in four weight classes. *Ring Magazine*'s Fighter of the Year in 1980 and 1984, Hearns, along with Marvin Hagler and Sugar Ray Leonard, dominated boxing during the 1980s, and his one-punch knockout of Roberto Duran, in 1984, sealed his legacy as a dominating puncher.

*"I hit him so hard in the first round. After that, I was so tired, it didn't really take all that much to put me down."*

The Hearns-Hagler bout in 1985 just might be the three best rounds in boxing history.

**Emmanuel Steward, trained, 1971-2012,** began his training career at the Kronk Recreation Center, turning it into a world respected gym. One of the greatest trainers in history, Emanuel taught Detroit's youth the lessons of determination and perseverance through boxing for decades.

*"I went to a motivational training course once, a course of self-discovery, and I found out after a week that my fear – it was not a fear of not being accepted – was a very violent fear of failure."*

*"If there is one abiding theme in the gym, it's the withering work in the ring. Those not fit do not survive."*

Throughout Steward's Hall of Fame career, he managed 41 champions, beginning with Hilmer Kenty and Tommy "Hitman" Hearns. His heavyweight fighters, including Lennox Lewis, had a record of 34-2-1 in title fights.

# ON POLITICS

*"Curse that little red dwarf. I hate the Nain Rouge!"*
- Antoine de la Mothe Cadillac, Explorer

I have known many politicians. Too many put their own self-interest above the interest of those they are supposed to represent. But there are a few good ones too. Detroit's certainly seen both kinds.

**Antoine de la Mothe Cadillac (1658-1730), Founder of Detroit, (1701-1710),** was a pompous, inept and utterly corrupt individual. He sought fame and wealth in Detroit and when things fell apart, he blamed me for his failings.

*"Detroit ruined me."*

Those were his dying words back in France. Cadillac's achievements include being stripped of his false titles, arrested, and sent back to France, bankrupt. This was the beginning of my reputation. Just don't fuck with me…

**Harry Hamilton (1734-1796), Lieutenant Governor and Superintendent of Indian Affairs, (1775-1779),** was a notorious Governor of Fort Detroit during the Revolutionary War. Seeking to control expansion into the Michigan territory, Hamilton granted land to those who swore allegiance to the King. For those who claimed to be from the Colonies, he paid the local Indian tribes for their scalps.

*"I'll pay you two shillings for every scalp you collect off anyone who doesn't swear allegiance to the Crown."*

His cruelty towards early settlers around Detroit earned him the nicknames "The Hair Buyer of Detroit" and "The Hair-Buyer General." In 1779, he was captured and made a prisoner of war by George Rogers Clark.

**George Rogers Clark (1752-1818), Soldier,** in 1778, was fighting the Revolutionary War in the West, and could've taken the Great Lakes from the British, thereby changing the war, if properly supplied. He remarked on the denial of his request for more troops:

*"Never was a person more mortified than I was at the time, to see so fair an opportunity to push a victory; Detroit lost for want of a few men."*

I told George Washington that he could have the entire West and Canada if he could take Detroit. Clark was a fierce proponent for my position, but Washington didn't believe in us.

**William Hull (1753-1825), Governor, Michigan Territory (1805-1812),** lost Detroit to the British and their Indian allies, led by Tecumseh, at the beginning of the War of 1812, without firing a shot. Fooled into believing he was surrounded by overwhelming forces, Hull surrendered Detroit to a much smaller army.

*"These Indians are more greedy of violence… than the Vikings or Huns."*

*"I give it all up."*

With rumors that General Hull had been drinking heavily prior to the surrender, and because of his timidity facing the enemy, Hull was court-martialed and sentenced to death. His cowardice was a major embarrassment for the young country.

**Gabriel Richard (1767-1832), St. Anne's Priest (1804-1832) and Founder of the University of Michigan,** arrived in Detroit in 1804 as assistant pastor at St. Anne's Church. After the Great Fire of

1805, which destroyed the entire city, Father Richard wrote the city's motto – *Speramus meliora; resurget cineribus*.

*"We hope for better things; it will arise from the ashes."*

Imprisoned by the British after the surrender of Fort Detroit, Richard refused to swear an oath of allegiance to his captors. Chief Tecumseh, who knew him to be a good man, refused to fight the Americans during his imprisonment, thus enabling his freedom.

*"I have taken an oath to support the Constitution of the United States and I cannot take another. Do with me as you please."*

After the war, I assisted Richard and Judge Woodward in founding the Catholepistemiad of Michigania in 1817, and in 1821 it became the University of Michigan.

**Augustus B. Woodward (1774-1827), First Chief Judge of Michigan (1805-1827),** adopted L'Enfant's street plan for Washington DC after the 1805 Fire leveled Detroit. Following existing Indian Trails,

Woodward Avenue was once called Court House Avenue. Responding to critics who decried the Woodward Avenue name, he remarked:

*"Maybe because it heads to the woods…"*

His decision in 1807 as Chief Judge freed two slaves who escaped from Windsor, Canada. He declared:

*"Any man coming into this Territory is by law of the land a freeman."*

Woodward, along with Father Richard and Lewis Cass, were men of vision in my mind. Without these men, Detroit would be a different place, as would Michigan.

**Lewis Cass (1782-1866), Territorial Governor of Michigan (1813-1831) and Senator (1845-1857),** is considered the father of the State of Michigan. His leadership led to Michigan becoming a state in 1837. He was elected Senator in 1845, serving Michigan until 1857.

*"Men may doubt what you say, but they will believe what you do."*

One of the great men who made Michigan, a fierce advocate for Detroit and a good friend, Cass had the shoulders that we all stood on to become a state.

**Hazen Pingree (1840-1901), Shoemaker,** said this in 1889 when asked to run for Mayor:

*"I'm too busy making shoes."*

**Hazen Pingree (1840-1901), Mayor (1890-97) and Governor (1897-1901),** took office during one of the great depressions in Detroit, yet he became one of the greatest mayors in American history. He was a voice for the disenfranchised.

*"Voter apathy was, and will remain the greatest threat to democracy."*

His contributions to Detroit are legendary. He donated much of his own money to pay for seeds to create urban farms and saved the starving residents of Detroit during the depression of 1890, earning the nickname Ol' Potato Patch Pingree.

**Damon Keith (1922- ), Judge, U.S. Sixth Court of Appeals (1977-1995),** was a civil rights legend and a key leader following the 1967 race riots.

*"Democracies die behind closed doors… When government begins closing doors, it selectively controls information rightfully belonging to the people."*

*"Selective information is misinformation."*

Judge Keith is best known for his rulings against Nixon's illegal wire taps and Bush's Attorney General John Ashcroft's secretive deportations after 9/11. Only his advocacy for his fellow Detroiters exceeds his successes as a judge.

**John F. Kennedy (1917-1963), President (1961-1963),** said this in his 1960 Labor Day Speech in Detroit, a precursor to his famous Inauguration speech:

*"The new frontier is not what I promise I am going to do for you. The new frontier is what I ask you to do for your country."*

*"The goals of the labor movement are the goals for all Americans and their enemies are the enemies of progress."*

*"American labor has insisted upon, and won, the*

*highest wages and best working conditions in the world. You have not been content to sit still and let well enough alone. You have shown that high living standards can be won within the context of freedom."*

I marched with JFK in the 1960 parade and told him he was going to be a great president. He was full of life and brought a new spirit to the country. The middle class started in Detroit through the power of the unions. As the unions have become marginalized, so has the middle class.

**George Romney (1907-1995), Governor (1963-1969),** was a progressive Republican at a time when political parties worked together to solve societies problems. A Mormon, he was very aware of the relationship of religion and politics.

*"Extremism in defense of liberty is not a vice, but I denounce political extremism, of the left or the right, based on duplicity, falsehood, fear, violence and threats when they endanger liberty."*

*"The rights of some must not be enjoyed by denying the rights of others. Neither can we permit states' rights at the expense of human rights."*

*"I'm concerned about truth and credibility in government."*

His leadership in advocating for racial equality was instrumental in bring about change. I wish politicians still felt this way. I'm not sure where his son went wrong.

**Jerome Cavanagh (1928-1979), Mayor (1962-1970),** brought with him the young charm of JFK and tried mightily to deliver change and growth to the city.

*"We hoped against hope that what we had been doing was enough to prevent a riot. It was not enough."*

*"What will it profit this country if we... put our man on the Moon by 1970 and at the same time you can't walk down Woodward Avenue in this city without fear of some violence?"*

I was a great admirer, and was sad to see the events of 1967 effectively end a promising career. Sensing the tensions of race and violence, the Mayor recognized that Detroit was in a battle bigger than itself and it was going to come at a steep price.

**Coleman Young (1918-1997), UAW Member,** was a powerful union activist and this was his response, in 1952, to the House Un-American Activities Committee led by McCarthy.

*"I am not here to fight in any un-American activities, because I consider the denial of the right to vote to large numbers of people all over the South, Un-American…"*

*"It is my contention you would not be in Congress today if it were not for the legal restrictions on voting on the part of my people…"*

*"I can assure you I have had no part in the hanging or bombing of Negroes in the South. I have not been responsible for firing a person from his job for what I think are his beliefs, or what somebody thinks he believes in, and things of that sort. That is the hysteria that has been swept up by this committee."*

As an accused communist, Coleman Young was called before the House Un-American Committee to answer for his political beliefs. Coleman tore down the committee with scathing attacks at the hypocrisies embedded in their witch hunt. He made his name as an activist and civil rights hero throughout the country but never more so than in Detroit, where the black population had a limited voice and were restricted in housing and job opportunities.

**Coleman Young (1918-1997), Mayor (1974-1994),** led Detroit through a bitter racially divisive period, witnessing the loss of almost half a million residents during his tenure. Never shy about his belief that the country was suffering from racial inequality, he was an outspoken leader, illuminating the hidden prejudices and outward activities of those who used race as a tactic for wielding power.

*"Racism is like high blood pressure – the person who has it doesn't know he has it until he drops over with a God damned stroke. There are no symptoms of racism. The victim of racism is in a much better position to tell you whether or not you're a racist than you are."*

*"I'm smiling all the time. That doesn't mean a God damned thing except I think people who go around solemn-faced and quoting the Bible are full of shit."*

Despite having a good relationship with the press, he continued to engage them with his own acerbic attitude.

*"Aloha, Mother Fuckers! – to the media while vacationing in Hawaii."*

Upon winning the election in a highly contentious contest between races, he made it clear to all who would not accept his leadership that they were no longer welcome in Detroit.

*"I issue a warning to all those pushers, to all rip-off artists, to all muggers: It's time to leave Detroit; hit 8 Mile. And I don't give a damn if they are black or white, or if they wear Super fly suits or blue uniforms with silver badges. Hit the road."*

Although he will be remembered primarily for his confrontational attitude, Mayor Young was not the bombastic despot that many have portrayed him in his final years. These are some of his more inspiring quotes.

*"Courage is one step ahead of fear."*

*"We must take the profit out of prejudice."*

*"We need to dream big dreams, propose grandiose means if we are to recapture the excitement, the vibrancy, and pride we once had."*

*"You can't look forward and backward..."*

Later in his Mayoral terms, he was accused of many abuses of power. This is his reaction to the police chief being indicted for trading banned South African Krugerrands.

***"I don't know nothing about no God Damned Krugerrands."***

I have to finish with the following quote as it sums up his distinct oratorical style. The man had quite the talent for foul language, and you know those who swear are more trustworthy.

***"Swearing is an art form. You can express yourself much more exactly, much more succinctly, with properly used curse words."***

Depending upon who you ask, Young was either a great leader or a bitter blowhard who exploited race in politics. My impression of him has always been mostly positive. He became mayor at the most contentious time in our history and, despite many achievements, could not eradicate racism and classism. Like many idolized leaders, he fell on his own sword, succumbing in his later years to favoritism and graft.

**Kwame Kilpatrick (1970- ), Mayor (2002-2008),** was elected with youthful promise, but lost himself to youthful arrogance. After creating an Imperial Court, Kwame robbed the poor, and fiddled while Detroit burned.

*"Detroit's been the butt of a lot of jokes for 50 years. We want to introduce the world to the new Detroit."*

*"My dream in growing up in the city of Detroit was to be Mayor. At the family picnics from the time I was 9-years-old that's what I told people I was going to be. The mayor of the city of Detroit."*

*"I don't think there has been any mayor in America scrutinized that way. I don't think there has been any mayor as a matter of fact, Coleman Young I think received an incredible amount of scrutiny and he was kind of the poster child for that in Detroit. He was the first Black mayor who really expressed his manhood in a different way than had been seen from African-American men that was projected across the country."*

Elected with an abundance of hope, he failed us all miserably, extending the Detroit jokes for years to come. Being raised in a political family with entitlements will make you think you're destined for something you're clearly not worthy of. But his remarks on Mayor Young are correct: Young was a polarizing figure in a polarizing time.

**Kevin D. Williamson (1972- ), *National Review* Correspondent,** is another of a long line of conservative writers inclined to attack the impoverished. But his take on the Kilpatrick administration was spot on.

*"Detroit's political leadership is a parasite that has outgrown its host."*

It's hard to argue with this sentiment when our Mayor, City Council Members, and a host of school administrators went to jail. It's a shame that people let politicians exercise such blatant self-interest.

**Daniel L. Doctoroff (1958- ), Businessman and Government Official,** was born in suburban Detroit and went on to become Deputy Mayor of New York City under Michael Bloomberg.

*"I believe that Detroit has a terrific geographical position. It still is a hub of one of the most important industries in the world. There's incredible engineering and other talent."*

Starting out as an Investment Banker at Lehman Brothers, Doctoroff joined the Bloomberg administration in 2008 focusing on rebuilding the city's infrastructure.

**Sander Levin (1931- ), Congressman,** a graduate of Detroit's Central High School, has served more than three decades in Congress representing Detroit.

*"My brother and late sister and I were raised in Detroit; it was where the middle class across racial lines, the middle class was able to develop, build a home, have for the first-time retirement benefits, have a job, and yes, their kids began to go to college."*

Coming from a family of great statesman, many Levin family members have sought government service.

**Carl Levin (1934- ), Senator,** was City Council President before becoming a U.S. Senator in 1978. He retired in 2015.

*"The Constitution is a document that should only be amended with great caution."*

*"We have a hope of succeeding if we learn from our past mistakes and pull together to make the hard choices."*

*"The American people deserve a budget that invests in the future, protects the most vulnerable among us and helps to create jobs and economic security."*

A truly remarkable man, Levin has dedicated most of his life to government service. For a time, I used to deliver the *Detroit News* to him when he lived in the Green Acres neighborhood of Detroit.

**Manuel "Matty" Maroun (1927- ), Transportation Industrialist,** has found every way to take advantage of a disabled city government by buying off politicians and exploiting loopholes for his personal benefit.

*"For me to own land in Detroit, it was a badge of honor, and it was support for the city."*

His two biggest crimes are overseeing the total dismantling of the Michigan Central Train Station and forever delaying the Gordie Howe Bridge. Scum, in my esteemed estimation.

**John Engler (1948- ), Governor, (1991-2003),** did much to damage Detroit. He signed multiple laws limiting the city's rights to enact its own laws and cut state financial support, leading to bankruptcy.

*"I wish we could've acted quicker on Detroit or other failing schools."*

*"I care about the children of Detroit."*

Engler systematically dismantled the public schools in Detroit. Decades later, we are still reeling from his handiwork.

**Ronald Reagan (1911-2004), President (1981-1989),** said in his 1980 acceptance speech at the GOP Convention in Detroit:

*"The American people – the American people – the most generous on earth, who created the highest standard of living, are not going to accept the notion that we can only make a better world for others by moving backward ourselves."*

I think he did try to take us backward, to a time before unions and a strong middle class.

**Robert Reich (1946- ), Labor Secretary in the Clinton Administration (1993-1997),** is a brilliant professor and economist. He understood the benefits unions brought to the middle class in Detroit and around the country.

*"Detroit is really a model for how wealthier and whiter Americans escape the costs of public goods they'd otherwise share with poorer darker Americans."*

I couldn't say it better myself. A city is complex and needs economic diversity to survive.

**Harry Reid (1939- ), Senator, NV, Senate Majority Leader (2007-2015),** helped create the Federal government's bailout plan for the auto industry.

*"Some said he shouldn't save Detroit. But President Obama made the tough and right call to save more than a million American jobs in an important, iconic industry."*

Without the auto bailout, Detroit would've lost its identity.

**John Boehner (1947- ), Speaker of the House (2011-2015),** led the U.S. House of Representatives during the auto bailout.

*"I think that the Detroit auto industry is important to the United States. It's important for hundreds of thousands of Americans who have their jobs as a result."*

From Ohio, Boehner had as many constituents invested in the auto industry as Michigan did.

**Rand Paul (1963- ), 2016 GOP Presidential Candidate,** responded to the 2015 State of the Union address with insights like this:

*"Although I was born into the America that experiences and believes in opportunity, my trips to Ferguson, Detroit, Atlanta and Chicago have revealed that there is an undercurrent of unease."*

No shit! Opportunities, jobs and education have suffered racial bias for centuries, but as Detroit became less diversified, ghettoization took hold and opportunities disappeared.

**Jeb Bush (1953- ), 2016 GOP Presidential Candidate,** was beaten badly by Trump, who connected with many average citizens (white ones, anyway), while Jeb suffered from his brother George's failures as president.

*"I think Detroit would do well if we started repopulating it with young, aspirational people."*

What is he even talking about? There are 700,000 people living in Detroit. Are we the forgotten masses?

**Ben Carson (1951- ), 2016 GOP Presidential Candidate,** became a famous neurosurgeon before running for office. The native Detroiter's lack of communication skills were his undoing.

*"I grew up in Detroit. I grew up in an environment where you were supposed to be Democrat, where they told you that Republicans were evil people and that they were racist."*

Despite his impressive success as a surgeon, Ben is totally disconnected from reality. I fear what he may do if given any substantial power.

**Mitt Romney (1947- ), 2012 GOP Presidential Candidate,** is another son of Detroit whose political career was derailed due to his disconnection from the average voter.

*"My father and I marched with Martin Luther King Jr. through the streets of Detroit."*

*"Let Detroit go bankrupt."*

His dad was a good man and I remember young Mitt growing up in Palmer Woods. His pandering for votes was too much for me though. A hometown boy who lost his soul.

**Rick Santorum (1958- ), 2012 and 2016 GOP Presidential Candidate,** is a right-wing Christian conservative whose main interest is returning us to the Stone Age.

*"Governor Romney supported the bailout of Wall Street and decided not to support the bailout of Detroit."*

To understand the disdain the left has for him, Google the definition of "Santorum."

**Donald Trump (1946- ), President,** won the 2016 Presidential election by enflaming fear and by promising control as well as jobs to a middle class devastated by government inaction.

*"You look at the inner cities, I just left Detroit, and I just left Philadelphia and I've met some of the greatest people I'll ever meet within these communities. And they are very, very upset with what their politicians have told them and what their politicians have done."*

At least he constructed a sentence.

**Milo Yiannopoulos (1984- ), Conservative Blogger,** is a troll who has never offered solutions but bitterly complains about government.

*"As a foreigner, I used to think all of Michigan was a post-apocalyptic wasteland of burning buildings, trashed cars, abandoned factories and broken dreams. But now I know that's just Detroit. It's only the Democrat-controlled areas that are a disaster."*

I put him in here reluctantly but hope that those who are familiar with him will respond to his hateful rhetoric and vitriol. I despise this one more than any other politician because at least they understand when to fake a righteous stance. This one seems to have no compassion or understanding of the world.

# ON RACE RELATIONS

*"Race always comes up in the conversation of Detroit."*
- Julie Mehretu, Artist

Issues of race have always been one of America's damning legacies. It has always confused and saddened me that people judge each other on such a simple human characteristic. As different as I am, I have experienced first-hand this bigotry. Initially it was the Indians, then Africans, Jews, Irish, Eastern Europeans, Hispanics and on and on… If everyone is considered an American, then why the bias? I would hope someday this country will recognize that.

**Tecumseh (1768-1813), Shawnee Chief,** was instrumental in the planning and capture of Fort Detroit, allied with the British, from General William Hull and the Americans. He came to be considered a national hero in Canada for the successful repulsion of the American invasion in 1812, which many Canadians believe led to their nationhood in 1867. He believed his alliance with the British would secure his homeland for the Shawnee. Unfortunately, he was manipulated and lied to, losing his life and his tribal home as expansion and annexation enveloped the Shawnee territories. So he knew a thing or two about betrayal. I once heard him say:

*"When Jesus Christ came upon the Earth, you killed Him. The son of your own God. And only after He was dead did you worship Him and start killing those who would not."*

Tecumseh also knew about courage and how to confront adversity – qualities I've often observed in Detroiters:

*"When your time comes to die, be not like those whose hearts are filled with fear of death, so that when their time comes they weep and pray for a little more time to live their lives over again in a different way. Sing your death song, and die like a hero going home."*

*"Show respect to all people, but grovel to none. Love your life, perfect your life, beautify all things in your life. A single twig breaks, but the bundle of twigs is strong."*

His oratory equaled his abilities as a great a military commander. I knew him for his love and passion to his tribe and for the greater Indian brotherhood. He dreamed of a Pan-Indian Confederation but died in battle.

**Zachariah Chandler (1813-1879), Senator,** was a prominent abolitionist, and one of the founders of the Republican Party. His hope was that,

*"One day blacks would be able to vote freely and safely, run for office, and make speeches throughout the nation, including the South, just as former rebels were allowed to vote, run for office, and speak in the North."*

Zach financially supported the Underground Railroad, advocated for Negro equality and was a fierce opponent of succession.

**Henry Bibb (1815-1854),** fled slavery to Detroit in 1842. In 1850, he published his autobiography *Narrative of the Life and Adventures of Henry Bibb, An American Slave,* which became one of the best-known slave narratives of the antebellum years. He hoped that…

*"This little volume will bear some humble part in lighting up the path of freedom and revolutionizing public opinion upon this great subject."*

After the Fugitive Act of 1850 was passed, Bibb fled to Windsor, Ontario, still active in the abolitionist movement.

**George DeBaptiste (1815-1875),** was the "president" of Detroit's Underground Railroad station and a former steward for President William Henry Harrison. On March 12, 1859, John Brown, Frederick Douglass, William Lambert, DeBaptiste, and I met at William Webb's house in Detroit. At the meeting, Brown's raid on Harper's Ferry was planned. DeBaptiste, frustrated with the pace of the abolitionist movement, proposed a more direct solution.

*"I believe we should send conspirators to blow up the South's largest churches."*

The suggestion was opposed by Brown, who believed that the idea was too aggressive.

**John Brown (1800-1859), Abolitionist,** first proposed his attack on the military garrison at Harper's Ferry, West Virginia, arming slaves to revolt against their masters while in Detroit.

*"Whereas, Slavery, throughout its entire existence in the United States is none other than a most barbarous, unprovoked, and unjustifiable War of one portion of its citizens upon another portion; the only conditions of which are perpetual imprisonment, and hopeless servitude or absolute extermination; in utter disregard and violation of those eternal and self-evident truths set forth in our Declaration of Independence."*

Fed up with the slow, non-violent, abolitionist approach. John remarked:

*"These men are all talk. What we need is action – action!"*

On the morning of December 2, 1859, before his execution, Brown wrote:

*"I, John Brown, am now quite certain that the crimes of this guilty land will never be purged away but with blood. I had, as I now think, vainly flattered myself that without very much bloodshed it might be done."*

Brown became a martyr of the fight for racial equality during the Civil War.

**Frederick Douglas (1818-1895),** became the leader of the Abolitionist movement. His 1845 autobiography, *Narrative of the Life of Frederick Douglass, an American Slave*, a bestseller, was extremely influential. These are a few of favorite quotes from him.

*"Opportunity is important but exertion is indispensable."*

*"Without a struggle, there can be no progress."*

Commenting on slavery's effects on education and development, he said:

*"It is easier to build strong children than to repair broken men."*

*"You are not judged by the height you have risen, but from the depth you have climbed."*

Douglass expressed his views on slavery and how it effects all of society this way:

*"Where justice is denied, where poverty is enforced, where ignorance prevails, and where any one class is made to feel that society is an organized conspiracy to oppress, rob and degrade them, neither persons nor property will be safe."*

Douglass called the meeting in Detroit with Brown and the Detroit leaders. He advocated for a more measured approach. I thought his approach was too reserved but his political acumen told him to go carefully.

**Laura Smith Haviland (1808-1898),** was considered a Superintendent on the Underground Railroad in Detroit. After freeing a family from Tennessee, in 1846, Haviland was pursued and harassed by the slave owners for 15 years.

*"I would not for my right hand become instrumental in returning one escaped slave to bondage. I firmly, believe in our Declaration of Independence, that all men are created free and equal, and that no human being has a right to make merchandise of others born in humbler stations, and place them on a level with horses, cattle, and sheep, knocking them off the auction-block to the highest bidder, sundering family ties, and outraging the purest and tenderest feelings of human nature."*

Havliland went on to work with Sojourner Truth at the Freedman's Hospital in Washington, DC. Once, a train conductor confronted Sojourner for riding as a black woman. Haviland intervened, allowing her to continue travelling.

*"Don't put her out, she belongs to humanity."*

Throughout her life, Haviland was active in seeking equal rights for blacks.

**Ossian Sweet (1895-1960),** was a Detroit doctor who moved into an all-white neighborhood in 1925, paying one-third more than the market value for his house. On the second night after moving in, Sweet invited nine others to protect him and his family. As crowds surrounded the home, rocks flew from the crowd. In retaliation, or self-defense, shots were fired from the second floor, killing one man. Sweet remarked:

*"Somewhere out there, standing among the women and children, lounging on the porches, lurking in the alleys were the men who would incite the crowd to violence."*

After the defense mounted by famed lawyer Clarence Darrow, the all-white jury found the defendants not guilty.

**Clarence Darrow (1918-2002),** defended Ossian Sweet and his family in court. His closing argument included details of the event but also insight regarding the state of racial equality in Detroit and the nation at the time.

*"My clients are charged with murder, but they are really charged with being black... You are facing a problem of two races, a problem that will take centuries to solve."*

*"I ask you gentleman in behalf of my clients... I ask you in behalf of yourselves, in behalf of our race to see that no harm comes to them. I ask you gentleman in the name of the future, the future which will one day solve these sore problems, and the future which is theirs as well as ours, I ask you in the name of the future to do justice in this case."*

The first trial ended in a mistrial. In the end, Darrow won acquittals for the Sweets as the entire nation focused on every trial detail.

**Charles Wright (1918-2002),** a Detroit obstetrician, opened his first museum of African-American culture in his medical offices on West Grand Blvd. in 1965.

*"My legacy was my job."*

*"I was committed to what I defined as 'one of the most important tasks of our times,' ensuring that generations, especially young African Americans, are made aware of and take pride in the history of their forbears and their remarkable struggle for freedom. An idea came to me that African-Americans needed a museum to collect and preserve our history and culture. And, with the help of many minds and hands, that idea came to fruition."*

Expanded and now located in the Cultural Center, the Charles H. Wright Museum of African-American history contains the largest permanent exhibit on African-American culture in the world. I visit often in my ongoing effort to comprehend America's history of racism.

**Elijah Muhammad (1897–1975), Nation of Islam Leader,** moved to Detroit from Georgia during the Great Migration of black people out of the South. Influenced by a speech on Islam and black empowerment, he joined Wallace D. Fard's group and eventually succeeded him and expanded the organization to more than 100 mosques nationwide and more than 20,000 members. Preaching his own version of Islam, he maintained that blacks were the "original" human being with whites being an offshoot race. He was determined to return the hegemony back to the black race. He dispensed words to live by like these:

*"Acquire knowledge. It enables its possessor to distinguish right from wrong; it lights the way to Heaven; it is our friend in the desert, our society in solitude, our companion when friendless; it guides us to happiness; it sustains us in misery; it is an ornament among our friends and an armor against enemies."*

*"There are three signs of a hypocrite: when he speaks he speaks lies, when he makes a promise he breaks it, and when he is trusted he betrays his trust."*

*"Four things support the world: the learning of the wise, the justice of the great, the prayers of the good, and the valor of the brave."*

*"Asking good questions is half of learning."*

I didn't always agree with all of his views, but I could understand how he became a highly influential mentor to such notable members as Malcolm X, Muhammad Ali, and Louis Farrakhan.

**Ralph Bunche (1904–1971), Civil Rights Leader,** a Detroit native, in 1950, became the first African-American to win the Nobel Peace Prize (for his efforts on the United Nations Palestine Commission in the 1940s). Bunche received the Medal of Freedom in 1963 from President John Kennedy. He was at the March on Washington and the march to Selma. Here are just a few of the things I learned from conversations with him:

*"I have a deep-seated bias against hate and intolerance. I have a bias against racial and religious bigotry. I have a bias that leads me to believe in the essential goodness of my fellow man, which leads me to believe that no problem of human relations is ever insoluble."*

*"Peace is no mere matter of men fighting or not fighting. Peace, to have meaning for many who have known only suffering in both peace and war, must be translated into bread or rice, shelter, health, and education, as well as freedom and human dignity – a steadily better life. If peace is to be secure, long-suffering and long-starved, forgotten peoples of the world, the underprivileged and the undernourished, must begin to realize without delay the promise of a new day and a new life."*

*"Hearts are the strongest when they beat in response to noble ideals."*

A contributor in the formation of the United Nations, Bunche was always seeking peaceful resolutions to conflict.

**Walter Reuther (1907-1970), UAW Leader,** was a socialist and fervent believer in the rights of workers of all colors. Surviving two assassination attempts, Reuther led strikers against Ford security in the "Battle of the Overpass," seeking to unionize Ford Motor Company.

*"There is no greater calling than to serve your fellow men. There is no greater contribution than to help the weak. There is no greater satisfaction than to have done it well."*

*"There is no power in the world that can stop the forward march of free men and women when they are joined in the solidarity of human brotherhood."*

Walter was active in the civil rights movement, attending the March on Washington and the Selma to Montgomery March. He stood beside Martin Luther King during his "I Have a Dream" speech, which I'd heard an earlier version of in Detroit.

**Grace Lee Boggs (1915–2015), Social Activist,** was one of Detroit's most influential muckrackers. She worked tirelessly for racial and gender equality. The Boggs Center to Nurture Community Leadership was formed in the 1990s by her supporters to continue her work in social activism. She knew that while race was always part of Detroit's story, it was never the whole story:

*"I think of what's happening in Detroit as part of something that's much bigger. Most people think of the decline of the city as having to do with African-Americans and being in debt, and all the issues like crime and bad housing. But what happened is that when globalization took place, following World War II, Detroit's role as the center and the symbol of industrialization was destroyed. It wasn't because we had black citizens mainly or a black mayor; it was because the world was changing."*

Grace unsuccessfully attempted to convince Malcolm X to run for the United States Senate in 1964.

**Malcolm X (1925-1965), Civil Rights Leader,** was known as "**Detroit Red**" and was running street hustles when I first met him. Joining Elijah Muhammad's Nation of Islam movement pulled him from the streets and turned him into one of the greatest racial advocates of the time. But his view of the NOI leader changed over time:

*"The thing that you have to understand about those of us in the Black Muslim movement was that all of us believed 100 percent in the divinity of Elijah Muhammad. We believed in him. We actually believed that God, in Detroit by the way, that God had taught him and all of that. I always believed that he believed in himself. And I was shocked when I found out that he himself didn't believe it."*

Malcolm became associated with the phrase "by any means necessary," with which he called to those who were discouraged with the progress of the non-violent movement. It has become a lasting statement to the fight for equality:

*"When you hear me say 'by any means necessary,' I mean exactly that. I believe in anything that is necessary to correct unjust conditions-political, economic, social, physical, anything that is necessary."*

He knew that fight was a long one and that progress would not be immediate:

*"If you stick a knife nine inches into my back and pull it out three inches, that is not progress. Even if you pull it all the way out, that is not progress. Progress is healing the wound, and America hasn't even begun to pull out the knife."*

Malcolm was an expert at turning an insightful, memorable phrase. Here are just some of the others I heard him say:

*"A wise man can play the part of a clown, but a clown can't play the part of a wise man."*

*"If you don't stand for something you will fall for anything."*

*"You and I have never seen democracy – all we've seen is hypocrisy."*

Malcolm stood out as one of the great leaders during the Civil Rights Movement.

**Martin Luther King Jr. (1929-1968), Civil Rights Leader,** first gave a version of his famous "I Have a Dream" speech in June 1963 at Detroit's "The Walk to Freedom" rally, the largest civil rights demonstration up to that date. In it, he said (among so many other highly quotable things):

*"And so, this afternoon, I have a dream. It is a dream deeply rooted in the American dream… With this faith, we will be able to achieve this new day when all of God's children, black men and white men, Jews and Gentiles, Protestants and Catholics, will be able to join hands and sing with the Negroes in the spiritual of old: Free at last! Free at last! Thank God almighty, we are free at last!"*

King was one of the greatest orators of all time, I believe. I marched with him on Woodward Avenue that day and was amazed at the outpouring of love and brotherhood. It was one of Detroit's greatest moments.

**Rosa Parks (1913-2005), Civil rights Activist,** has been called "the mother of the freedom movement" for her heroic resistance on a bus in Montgomery Alabama, in 1955, refusing to give up her seat to a white passenger. Parks moved to Detroit soon after, and briefly served Congressman John Conyers in Washington, DC.

*"Racism is still with us. But it is up to us to prepare our children for what they have to meet, and, hopefully, we shall overcome."*

*"Memories of our lives, of our works and our deeds will continue in others."*

*"As far back as I can remember, I knew there was something wrong with our way of life when people could be mistreated because of the color of their skin."*

*"I would like to be remembered as a person who wanted to be free... so other people would be also free."*

Rosa Parks was a respected leader in the civil rights movement. Remaining active in social justice, she formed the Rosa and Raymond Parks Institute for Self-Development, which runs the "Pathways to Freedom" tours, introducing students to important civil rights and Underground Railroad sites.

**John Conyers (1929- ), Congressman,** has served in the House of Representatives, representing Detroit since 1965. He is a founding member of the Congressional Black Caucus.

*"We still have a huge inner-city problem in Detroit – of housing, homelessness, joblessness, an incredibly decrepit education system, high crime rates, drug abuse, welfare dependency, teen-age pregnancy."*

During the 1967 riots, Conyers was one of two black Congressman from Detroit, Charles Diggs, the other. With only a total of four black Representatives in Congress, Detroit's Congressmen equaled 50% of all African-American representation throughout the nation at the time.

**Dennis Archer (1942- ), Mayor (1994–2001),** was a former Michigan Supreme Court Justice. Archer succeeded Coleman Young as Mayor.

*"Whatever damage you inflict to your own city, it is likely to remain permanent, because in the very same areas where there used to be flourishing businesses, they do not exist today, and in the very same areas where there used to be dense housing units, they no longer exist today."*

Although Archer did his best to bring integrity back to the office, his opponents, mostly loyalists of Young, fought against him. He is credited with taking steps to repair the long divisions between the city and suburbs after Young.

**Charlie LeDuff (1960- ), Pulitzer Prize –Winning Writer,** is Detroit through and through: gruff and confrontational, yet intelligent. Although it's been a few years, we used to golf occasionally and if I remember right, he offered good advice on my game. His book *Detroit: An American Autopsy* is a fascinating read. Some of what he says about the city, I first heard him say out on the links. Things like this:

*"The city belongs to the black man. The white man was a convenient target until there were no white men left in Detroit. What used to be black and white is now gray. Whites got the suburbs and everything else. The black machine's got the city and the black machine's at war with itself. The spoils go to the one who understands that."*

*"In Detroit, we all talked the race game. It is a way of life."*

Known for his acerbic wit and his support of Detroit's firefighters, Charlie was a TV icon for a few years.

**John G. Rodwan Jr. (1968-  ), Essayist,** is a more obscure writer than Charlie, but one with plenty of experience of our shared city:

*"Growing up in Detroit when I did among the people I knew taught me that it makes no sense to think all black people think and behave the same way and*

*that all white people think and behave the same way – no matter how much folks from inside and outside the city insisted so. The city's story is more complicated – and interesting – than that. So are its people."*

John is a writer and a friend, and we've spent a lot of time discussing the future of Detroit, as well as its past.

## On the '43 Riots

Racial tensions were building as the "Great Migration", southern families, both black and white, tripled Detroit's population to 1.6 million in 1940. Seeking jobs in the lucrative auto industry, they also brought with them their racial prejudices.

**Anonymous Black Citizen,** remarked about the lack of housing and that a federal housing project, The Sojurner Truth Project, was going to house white people instead of the promise to create more black homes.

*"The Army is going to take me to 'fight for democracy,' but I would just as soon fight for democracy right here. Here we are fighting for ourselves."*

The government reversed its decision, allowing blacks to move in to the new community, in 1942. This was the precursor to the extreme tensions surrounding race, income inequality, and restricted opportunities for African-Americans in Detroit during this time.

After the U.S. entered World War II, the government demanded that manufacturing facilities start producing war materials. For Detroit, no more cars would be produced until the wars end. Although the UAW hierarchy supported integration, the rank and file did not. Whites refused to work side by side with blacks. Three weeks before the riots, Packard assigned three black workers to work next to white workers, igniting a plant-wide strike. 25,000 white workers walked off the job. Over the loudspeakers, a voice shouted:

*"I'd rather see Hitler and Hirohito win than work next to a Nigger."*

**Edward Jeffries, Mayor (1940-1948),** a supporter of racial integration, understood that Detroit was on the edge, that any incident could become a riot. On Sunday, June 20, 1943, after years of tension, fights broke out between two groups on the Belle Isle Bridge. Black teenagers, led by "Little Willie," who previously had been harassed by a group of white teens, vowed revenge. This sparked a city-wide riot. Thousands of whites attempted to invade Black Bottom, the center of black life in Detroit. Jeffries declared over the radio:

*"Our enemies could not have accomplished as much by a full-scale bombing raid. I appeal to the good citizens of Detroit to keep off the streets, keep in their homes or at their jobs."*

An emergency call led Dr. Joseph De Horatiis to Paradise Valley, a black section of Detroit. Warned by police not to cross the roadblock, he walked into the neighborhood, answering the call, where he was beaten to death by a mob. The eulogy by **Father Hector Saulino**, offered a reminder to us all:

*"In his death Dr. De Horatiis offers a solution to all wars – Christian charity. When will the world learn that as long as men beat one another and strive greedily and selfishly against each other, peace cannot return to stay?"*

A day into the riot, the white mobs again assailed Black Bottom, protected by a police line. Officer Lawrence Adams, caught in the cross fire, was shot and killed. **Reverend Brestidge** remarked:

*"He was the victim of the hate of man, which has replaced the love of God in the hearts of too many of us."*

In front of the Detroit Library, the National Guard encountered almost 15,000 white rioters, roaming unabated and beating any blacks they encountered. **Colonel Krech** ordered his men:

*"Fix your bayonets, load your guns and don't take anything from anyone."*

The mob scattered. By midnight, the authorities had restored order. Commenting on the city's preparedness, **Mayor Jeffries** said:

*"We were greenhorns in this area of race riots, but we are greenhorns no longer. We are veterans now. We will not make the same mistakes again."*

The 1943 Riots were one of many Detroit experienced in its history, but until this time, none were as devastating. The entire city seemed awash with racial hatred. White mobs roamed the streets and encircled black neighborhoods. Unlike the 1967

Rebellion, this riot was led primarily by the white population of Detroit against their black neighbors.

**Aftermath:**
**Dead - 34**
**Injured - 675**
**Arrested - 1,895**
**Damage - $2,000,000**

## On the '67 Rebellion

During the three years prior to summer 1967, more than 300 race riots had broken out across the nation. Detroit seemed to have avoided the rising racial tensions that other cities experienced. A month before the Detroit Rebellion, **H. Rap Brown**, gave a speech at the four-day "Black Arts Convention" at the Shrine of the Black Madonna, home to Detroit's black separatist movement, led by **Reverend Albert Cleage**. Brown said:

*"Let white America know that the name of the game is tit-for-tat, an eye for an eye, a tooth for a tooth, and a life for a life. Motown, if you don't come around, we are going to burn you down!"*

After the assassination of Malcom X, H. Rap Brown

became the voice for the more outspoken black community.

Reverend Cleage, a fiery orator, and proponent for Black independence, created the idea of a "Black Nation." He observed:

*"At every meeting, some young black man jumps to his feet screaming, 'I can't stand it any longer. Let's take to the streets and get it over with!' We all know how he feels and why he feels that way. Each of us has felt that same sense of powerlessness that makes us ache with helplessness and hopelessness and drives us to seek death as an easy way out. Those of us who cry out think of ourselves as revolution-ists and participants in the Black Revolution. But a revolution seeks to change conditions. So, each day we must decide. Either we are trying to achieve the power to change conditions or we have turned from the struggle and are seeking a heroic moment when we can die in the streets."*

In the 1950s, the original black neighborhoods were wiped out, Black Bottom was razed for urban renewal, and the Chrysler Freeway was built over Hastings Street. As housing restrictions against blacks abated,

12<sup>th</sup> Street, became the new Main Street for Black Life. It was nicknamed, the Sin Strip, Avenue of Fun or the Pocket Ghetto.

**Anonymous,** describing 12<sup>th</sup> Street at night:

*"There was a daytime 12<sup>th</sup> Street, and there was a nighttime 12<sup>th</sup> Street, and they didn't overlap. During the day, the good citizens came out like your mother. All the hustlers that were out there knew that your mother wasn't into that stuff, so she just came shopping. But come dark, mama goes home, gets off the street, and the night shift comes on."*

*"12<sup>th</sup> Street is a place where a black man with a little money in his pocket can go and try to forget he's black."*

Saturday night, July 22, 1967, was hot and steamy. Above the Economy Printing Company, in a known after-hours club, Bill Scott was hosting a party for two Vietnam vets. About 11pm, two undercover officers attempted to enter the party. The **Doorman** opened the peephole, and, not recognizing them responded:

*"We don't know you."*

According to **Patrolman Henry**, one of the black undercover officers, who later became a police commander, the clubs were friendly gatherings.

*"I had trouble getting in. There was a pool table they'd used to shoot dice, a bar, a kitchen that served food. It looked like a third-rate bar. People were having a good time. There were different circumstances in those days. People were friendlier, they would drink and gamble, but there was very little dope. Customers had no fear of a jail sentence. Especially in the 10th Precinct, along Twelfth Street [a police raid] was a common occurrence."*

After attempting to infiltrate other known after hour clubs, the officers returned at 3:30 am to try again. This time, the doorman let them in and the officers announced the raid. Paddy wagons rolled up, time and again, and everyone in the club was arrested. Crowds gathered as the prisoners were led to the wagons. Within minutes, the crowd grew into hundreds of onlookers. One young man, nicknamed "**Green Sleeves**" by police because of his green shirt, began shouting:

*"Black Power, don't let them take our people away; look what they are doing to our people... Let's kill*

*them whitey mother fuckers... let's get the bricks and bottles going. Why do they come down here and do this to our people?"*

Incited by "Green Sleeves," the crowd started harassing the police as they were rounding up the last of their prisoners. A bottle flew out from the crowd and pandemonium broke loose. The crowd raged down 12th Street, destroying and damaging anything they could. By 8 am, the crowd surged to over 10,000, a mixture of looters, onlookers and residents attempting to calm the situation. Sensing chaos, the police withdrew, hoping their withdrawal would calm the crowd. Hours later, Hardy Drugs, just doors away, was the first looted, and Sunday morning, at 6:30 am, the first fire was started. Ironically, Economy Printing, the origin of the Rebellion, escaped much of the riot's destruction as the surrounding streets were destroyed. As dawn led into day, and as the rioters grew in numbers, the devastation continued. Local black community leaders arrived, hoping to calm the growing insurrection. **Congressman John Conyers** took to the streets, jumped on top of a car, grabbed a bullhorn, and implored people to stop.

*"We're with you! But, please! This is not the way to do things! Please go back to your homes!"*

Ignoring his pleas, they responded by throwing bricks, bottles and rocks. Local legend and Detroit Tiger great Willie Horton walked through the crowds in his baseball uniform urging the rioters to relent to no avail. The riot continued throughout Monday, the looting and fires increased, and one **Black Merchant** remarked:

*"You were going to get looted no matter what color you were."*

There were over 231 incidents reported per hour, with almost 500 individual fires. Not even the Fire Department was spared, as rioters threw rocks and took shots as they tried to extinguish the blazes. One black store owner, **Mr. Perry**, commented:

*"It burned, it all burned, I didn't have one cent of insurance."*

Still in the neighborhood, Mr. Perry, remaining from the days of the riots, continues to operate a small store down the street from his original store. Much like the rioters, the police were indiscriminate in their ferocity in trying to restore order. The mostly white police force was accused of many horrendous actions during the riots.

**Officer Isaiah McKinnon,** who moved through the ranks to become Deputy Mayor, described one encounter as he was returning home after a 12-hour shift. Two white officers pulled him over and approached his vehicle, stopping him for violating the curfew. **McKinnon**, still in his police uniform, told the officers that he, too, was on the force.

*"The older guy, he had his gun out and he made a racially derogatory comment to me, I could see that he was pulling the trigger. I dove back into my car as he fired, and I just floored it."*

Despite the efforts of the police and National Guard, by Monday night, the riot was spreading across the city. Republican governor George Romney finally called President Lyndon B. Johnson to call out the Army. Even though Johnson had sent troops to quell uprisings in California, no help was given to Detroit. Instead, he sent **Cyrus Vance** as an envoy. Touring the affected areas, Vance said:

*"It doesn't look too bad to me."*

**Mayor Cavanagh** shot back:

*"Usually the city isn't burning."*

**President Johnson's** reluctance to send troops was due, in part, to his fear the media would:

*"Charge that we cannot kill enough people in Vietnam, so we go out and shoot civilians in Detroit."*

Assigning **U.S. Army Lt. General John L. Throckmorton** to Detroit, Johnson was updated hourly. Trying to assuage Johnson's concerns, Throckmorton told the President,

*"Mr. President, we will only shoot under the most severe provocations."*

When Throckmorton asked **Michigan National Guard General Cecil Simmons** what his orders were, Simmons replied:

*"We are to use as much force as necessary. If we are unable to stop them any other way, they will be shot."*

Throckmorton, shocked, countermanded Simmons's orders. **Simmons** responded,

*"You mean you want them to get away?"*

On July 27, the Rebellion ended. Twelfth Street was completely destroyed. An **assistant to Mayor Cavanagh** said:

*"It was mostly a rebellion against circumstances of a people who have no stake in society, people of both races. You put up with the status quo as long as it works for you. If you are going nowhere and there is no end in sight, then the hostility grows."*

**A.D. (1953- ), Pimp with a Limp,** saw first-hand the riots as a young boy and its effects have influenced him like many young black man of the time.

*"The community in the heart of Detroit answered a question the white power structure failed to ask… How big a mountain of oppression can a group of citizens endure before they erupt and explode? The people's answer exposed the darkness of intimidation and repudiated it with the torch of rebellion on the city."*

AD is a good friend and no one I know has experienced a more "Detroit" life than the one he lives.

**Jeffrey Eugenides (1960- ), Pulitzer Prize –Winning Novelist,** might have summed it up best when he said:

*"In Detroit, in July of 1967, what happened was no less than a guerrilla uprising."*

During those four days in Detroit, an estimated 10,000 people participated in the riots, while an additional 100,000 gathered to watch. Five decades later, there is still ample evidence that the Kerner Commission, an 11-member National Advisory Commission on Civil Disorders formed by President Johnson in response to the 1967 Detroit uprising, found that "our nation is moving toward two societies, one black, one white – separate and unequal."

*Aftermath:*
**Dead - 43**
**Injured - 1,189**
**Arrested - 7,200**
**Damage - $60,000,000**
**Stores Looted – 2,509**
**Homes Burned – 388**
**Buildings Destroyed – 2,000 +**

# CREDITS

Using many different media to assemble these quotes, these books, in particular, should be credited for their contributions. I found them engaging and great reads if you like Detroit. Please go out and get a copy for yourself.

*Black Detroit*, **Herb Boyd**

*Detroit Rock City*, **Steve Miller**

*Why Be Something That You're Not,* **Tony Rettman**

*Heaven Was Detroit*, **M.L. Liebler**

# THANKS

I would like to offer a special thanks to the following-

**John Rodwan**, for editing and polishing the words and content assembled here.

**Kiersten Armstrong and Mike Warlow at KMW Studio** for another outstanding job, assembling and designing this collection.

**Andy Wainio**, for being a great representative of the Nain Rouge.

**Andrea O'Donnell**, for her awesome makeup and design work.

**Jackson and Dylan Krieger**, for nothing really, other than to say that "I love them."